Palgrave Studies in the History of Economic Thought

Series Editors
Avi J. Cohen
Department of Economics
York University & University of Toronto
Toronto, ON, Canada

G. C. Harcourt
School of Economics
University of New South Wales
Sydney, NSW, Australia

Peter Kriesler
School of Economics
University of New South Wales
Sydney, NSW, Australia

Jan Toporowski
Economics Department,
SOAS University of London
London, UK

Palgrave Studies in the History of Economic Thought publishes contributions by leading scholars, illuminating key events, theories and individuals that have had a lasting impact on the development of modern-day economics. The topics covered include the development of economies, institutions and theories.

The series aims to highlight the academic importance of the history of economic thought, linking it with wider discussions within economics and society more generally. It contains a broad range of titles that illustrate the breath of discussions – from influential economists and schools of thought, through to historical and modern social trends and challenges – within the discipline.

All books in the series undergo a single-blind peer review at both the proposal and manuscript submission stages.

For further information on the series and to submit a proposal for consideration, please contact the Wyndham Hacket Pain (Economics Editor) wyndham.hacketpain@palgrave.com.

Mats Lundahl

Bo Södersten from Left to Right

Portrait of a Political Economist

Mats Lundahl
Stockholm School of Economics
Stockholm, Sweden

ISSN 2662-6578   ISSN 2662-6586 (electronic)
Palgrave Studies in the History of Economic Thought
ISBN 978-3-031-09100-1   ISBN 978-3-031-09101-8 (eBook)
https://doi.org/10.1007/978-3-031-09101-8

© The Author(s), under exclusive licence to Springer Nature Switzerland AG 2022
This work is subject to copyright. All rights are solely and exclusively licensed by the Publisher, whether the whole or part of the material is concerned, specifically the rights of translation, reprinting, reuse of illustrations, recitation, broadcasting, reproduction on microfilms or in any other physical way, and transmission or information storage and retrieval, electronic adaptation, computer software, or by similar or dissimilar methodology now known or hereafter developed.
The use of general descriptive names, registered names, trademarks, service marks, etc. in this publication does not imply, even in the absence of a specific statement, that such names are exempt from the relevant protective laws and regulations and therefore free for general use.
The publisher, the authors, and the editors are safe to assume that the advice and information in this book are believed to be true and accurate at the date of publication. Neither the publisher nor the authors or the editors give a warranty, expressed or implied, with respect to the material contained herein or for any errors or omissions that may have been made. The publisher remains neutral with regard to jurisdictional claims in published maps and institutional affiliations.

This Palgrave Macmillan imprint is published by the registered company Springer Nature Switzerland AG.
The registered company address is: Gewerbestrasse 11, 6330 Cham, Switzerland

Bo Södersten (1931–2017)

For Astrid and Birgit

Preface

During his entire professional career, Gunnar Myrdal insisted that economists are the slaves of hidden value premises, premises which govern our thinking and make it appear to be more objective than what it really is, value premises which bias our analysis. The remedy is obvious: make the value premises explicit, so the readers understand what kind of glasses to put on. I am writing about a person who was very close to me—and I don't intend to hide the fact that it is a person who influenced me much, in a way that I perceive as very positive. His name was Bo Södersten.

Bo made a statement which decided the course of the rest of my life: "Now, you'd better leave that goddamn business administration behind and get a PhD in economics!" I had arrived at Lund University in January 1966, studying Spanish for a semester before I began my studies of business administration and economics in the fall. Bo and I met in the fall of 1968 at the beginning of my last year of undergraduate studies. I was majoring in organization theory, writing a thesis about conflict resolution. At the same time, I needed to complete my degree with what in the contemporary student jargon was known as "the sixth credit." (Passing one semester's studies you obtained one credit in the system used at the time.) In my case, the "sixth credit" consisted of international economics, where the first half—international trade and international macroeconomics—was taught by Bo, then associate professor—a very enthusiastic Bo, who was in the process of writing his textbook, *International Economics*, and who offered his students enormously inspiring lectures. In the spring of 1969, the professor of international economics, Torsten Gårdlund, who taught the second half—development economics—brought the entire class to Tunisia, where he had worked as an economic advisor, a very stimulating experience. As a result, I signed for the "two-credit" level as well, where Bo also had a course.

During the summer of 1969, I had an AIESEC (Association Internationale des Étudiants en Sciences Économiques et Commerciales) internship with the small CIB Corporation in San Juan, Puerto Rico. When Bo heard that, he immediately told me: "Then you must go to Haiti as well!" He had been there himself in September 1968 and was intrigued by the country. I told him that he was battering in an open door, since I had already decided to do so. The visit to Haiti was something that I will never forget. It was when I came back home that Bo uttered the words that sealed my fate. The following year, he saw to it that I got some travel money which allowed me to return to Haiti and systematically collect material on the economy. I signed up for his "3-credit" level course in international economics and wrote a very long paper on the Haitian peasant economy, in 1971. Bo got me a contract to publish it commercially in Swedish. In the end, however, I did not do it. It became the starting point for my PhD dissertation instead.

Over the next few years, Bo and I collaborated on development issues, publishing a couple of anthologies and articles together. He sent me to India on a small-scale industry mission for the Swedish International Development Agency (SIDA) in 1971 and 1972, which he had been offered himself but was unable to accept. Bo also saw to it that I could spend the year 1975 at the Center for Latin American Development Studies at Boston University, headed by the grand old man of development economics, Paul Rosenstein-Rodan, when I was working on my doctoral dissertation. I followed Bo to Gothenburg and his chair in economics there in 1976 and then back to Lund again in 1978 (he had become professor of international economics there the year before). We ran the doctoral seminar in international economics and development together, and when I had defended my doctoral dissertation and Bo was elected to Parliament, in the fall of 1979, I had to substitute for him, as acting professor, until I got my own chair in development economics at the Stockholm School of Economics in 1987.

Ever since I met Bo, he and I were good friends—very good friends— and we saw a great deal of each other over the years both professionally and in the friends and family context, and when Bo's predecessor at Lund University, Torsten Gårdlund, died in 2003, we decided to write about him together, which in the end yielded a small book about his life and works.

Coming back to Gunnar Myrdal, the above should be kept in mind when reading the present book. It has been written by someone very positively predisposed toward his subject. The book could not have been written without various kinds of assistance from a number of people: Mats Bergstrand, Yves Bourdet, Henrik Braconier, Karolina Ekholm, Gunnar Eriksson, Kjell-Olof Feldt, Gunnar Fredriksson, Helena Frielingsdorf Lundqvist, Per-Axel Frielingsdorf, Birgit Friggebo, Tarmo Haavisto, Tobias Idberg, Lars Jonung, Anders Milton, Svante Nycander, Kristian Örnelius, Inga Persson, Jeanie and Lennart Petersson, Lars Pettersson, Lars Ramqvist, Robert Rydén, Nils-Eric Sandberg, Ann-Marie and Bo Sandelin, Fredrik Sjöholm, Anna, Astrid and Wiktor Södersten. I am grateful to all of them.

Stockholm, Sweden   Mats Lundahl
31 March 2022

Praise for *Bo Södersten from Left to Right*

"Mats Lundahl has written a wonderful book about one of the most charismatic Swedish intellectuals of the 20th century. Professor Bo Södersten made an imprint in different arenas of society. His career as an academic, which included many fierce academic fights, peaked with his famous textbook in international economics. As a politician he became Member of Parliament for the Social Democrats but failed to become a minister despite trying hard. Lundahl's book gives the reader an understanding of how the requirements for a political career differ from requirements in the academic world. Finally, Bo's career as a public intellectual, arguably his main contribution, is laid out in full. He was a prolific writer of newspaper articles and essays. Lundahl's book describes the many economic and political issues that Bo addressed with his sharp mind and pen. It is a treat to be reminded about the different policy issues that were both on the Swedish agenda over the years and on how well Bo managed to write about them. But the book is also about Sweden. It shows the social and economic development taking place in Sweden over a lifetime, through the work of a true intellectual who was very much part of the transition. I highly recommend this volume."
—Fredrik Sjöholm, *Professor of Economics and CEO at the Research Institute of Industrial Economics (IFN), Stockholm*

"In the official history of the University of Gothenburg, the years from 1971 to 1977 at the economics department, when Bo Södersten was professor there, are described as follows: 'The department of economics was characterized by strong ideological tensions. A group of students and teachers appeared who were strongly convinced that economics can be used for the achievement of a more fundamental and complete understanding of society. Several of them had a Marxist orientation.'

I was one of those who shared this 'Marxist orientation' and Bo Södersten was the protagonist of the opposite side in this conflict. Today, I have understood that his criticism was beneficial for us. We had to sharpen our arguments and make our criticism of mainstream economics more stringent.

Mats Lundahl has written a very thorough and lively story of my old favorite enemy Bo Södersten, a story which also brings to life the ideological march of the Swedish Social Democracy from Socialism to socially embedded capitalism."
—Johan Lönnroth, *Associate Professor Emeritus, Department of Economics, University of Gothenburg, Ex-Vice President of the Swedish Left Party*

"Some people's personalities are so strong that their effect on people around them lingers long after they are gone. Bo Södersten was such a person. He was born into a miner's family in the early 1930s but climbed the social ladder by becoming professor of economics, Member of Parliament and a prolific policy debater and essayist. Along the way, he upset many people with his sometimes ferocious attacks. But he also created deep friendships through his warmth, wit and strong loyalty. Mats Lundahl has written a wonderful book about this extraordinary person. He writes: 'Bo Södersten in a sense was larger than life. He was the kind of person that everybody loved to tell stories about, half of which cannot be printed.' Well, if you want to know the half that can be printed, you should read this book."
—Karolina Ekholm, *Professor of Economics, Stockholm University and Director General, Swedish National Debt Office*

Contents

1	Growing Up	1
2	Uppsala	9
3	Doctor	19
4	After the Dissertation	29
5	Essays	37
6	The Hunt for a Chair	45
7	The Housing Market	53
8	The Dream of the Labor-Managed Economy	59
9	Contrasting Economies: Sweden and the Developing Countries	69
10	Three Continents	77
11	In Parliament	85

12	The Debater	91
13	Saulus Falls off the Horse	99
14	The Overgrown Public Sector	105
15	Nuclear Power, Childcare, and Higher Education	113
16	Two Controversial Issues	119
17	Concentration of Power and Corruption	125
18	Systemic Defects	131
19	Book Reviews and Biography	137
20	Who Was He, Really?	145

| References | 163 |
| Index | 181 |

CHAPTER 1

Growing Up

Bo Södersten was born in Grängesberg in Dalarna in 1931. His family can be traced back to the early seventeenth century, to Västmanland, but at the end of the next century, it had moved to Dalarna. Bo's father, Wiktor, born in 1883, worked in the iron mine in Grängesberg. He was a trade union leader and a convinced and politically active Social Democrat. Wiktor was the head of the local mine workers' union, of which he was one of the founders, during the six-month Swedish mining strike in 1928, and he was subsequently on the board of the national federation of miners. In 1939, Wiktor became the chairman of the Grängesberg crisis board which handled the local wartime rationing.

In spite of having gone to school for a mere four years, Wiktor Södersten was a true intellectual who loved to read fiction, history, and philosophy, and who was engaged in the local library and the workers' educational association. He was on the board on the well-known Brunnsvik folk high school where adults could make up for lack of formal schooling. He was also a devote Christian and a very dominant person—Bo inherited his short temper from his father—who at the same time could irradiate warmth. Wiktor's strong political

© The Author(s), under exclusive license to Springer Nature Switzerland AG 2022
M. Lundahl, *Bo Södersten from Left to Right*, Palgrave Studies in the History of Economic Thought,
https://doi.org/10.1007/978-3-031-09101-8_1

Anna and Wiktor Södersten. (Courtesy Anna Södersten Bengtsson)

commitment provided a strong stimulus for his youngest son as well. Bo was born into the Swedish Social Democracy and was exposed to its ideology on an almost daily basis. This influence was to grow during more than five decades, until the mid-1980s. It would make him go into politics himself.

Swedish Society 1930–1970

Bo Södersten was born into a country which was undergoing a profound economic and social change.[1] The growth rate of the Swedish GDP for the period 1930–1951 was the highest in the world. The engineering and chemical industries were the leading sectors in the growth process, but the industrial sector as a whole grew with almost 5 percent per annum over this period while agriculture contracted. Sweden became an eminently industrial country. It weathered the depression of the 1930s comparatively well, because the gold standard was abandoned which made it possible for the Riksbank to stimulate the economy and because Swedish exports were not hit to the same extent as those of other Western countries.

---

[1] See Magnusson (1996), Chapters 11–13 and Schön (2000), Part 5, for overviews of the period.

During the Second World War, the industrial production was increasingly concentrated on the domestic market, notably on the market for basic consumer goods. The 1950s, in turn, were another decade of high growth and the Swedish standard of living rose to a level never experienced before. Exports and investment increased, and Sweden entered what would be labeled the "record years," a period which extended through the 1960s and the first years of the 1970s as well. Common people could afford to buy refrigerators, freezers, television sets, and cars to an increasing extent, and to travel abroad.

Hand in hand with the economic expansion went the creation of the Swedish welfare state. The growth of the material base made it possible to transfer some of the fruits of growth to low-income groups, both directly and indirectly through the expansion of education, health care, and other social services. Overall, the public sector expanded beyond the provision of collective goods into individual goods and services as well. The "Swedish model"—a mixed economy—was created and acquired worldwide fame. In the mid-1970s, Sweden had reached a living standard hitherto unheard of. This was the Swedish society that Bo Södersten grew up in, an increasingly prosperous society and an increasingly successful Social Democratic party.

There is no doubt whatsoever about the fact that the economic history of Sweden from the beginning of the 1930s to the mid-1970s had a profound impact on Bo Södersten. We will in the following have plenty of occasions to see how this history influenced his writings and actions, as a scientist, as a politician, and as a debater. The events of the period 1930–1975 constitute the backdrop especially for Bo's ideologically charged production. He was to a very large extent the child of his times and he did his best to interpret and analyze them during his entire professional life. The rest of the present work should be read with this in mind.

Childhood

Bo was the youngest of eight brothers and sisters, born ten years after his youngest brother. The children arrived during almost thirty years: Helmer (1903), Helge (1906), Alice (1909), Greta (1912), Sigrid (1916), Stig (1918), Erik (1921), and, with a ten-year lag, Bo (1931).

Wiktor, his wife Anna and their children, 1919. Back row, left to right: Wiktor, Helmer, Helge, Stig, Anna. Front row, left to right: Alice, Greta, Sigrid. (Courtesy Anna Södersten Bengtsson)

Wiktor, his wife, Anna, and their children lived in a one-room apartment in Laxtorp, a mineworker district, until 1938:

> Laxtorp, where I grew up, consisted of a number of working-class dwellings. In each house lived four families in apartments with one room and a kitchen and a relatively large closet. The houses were arranged in double rows and between the houses there was a street, one 'upper' and one 'lower' street. Altogether, at the time, there were around 20 to 30 houses, and some 100 families lived there, in a relatively small area. This of course meant that everybody knew each other. Everyone rented from the company and all of them worked in the mine or in some profession connected with it, mainly underground. You hence worked, dwelled and lived together, which meant that the extent of social control became exceedingly strong.[2]

Even though the oldest children had already left home, the small apartment could not house the entire Södersten family. Wiktor and Anna slept

---

[2] The quotation comes from the unfinished memoirs that Bo wrote between 1998 and 2001 (Södersten 2001a).

in the kitchen, Sigrid and Greta had to share a bed, and in the summer, Stig and Erik moved into the family woodshed and slept there—so Bo spent his first years, until he began school in 1938, with his oldest sister, Alice, and her husband, Henry Carlsson, later Ramqvist, the father of Lars Ramqvist, who would become the head of the Ericsson company. His first teacher was Märtha Nyström, the sister of the well-known Swedish composer Gösta Nystroem (who had internationalized his last, but not his first, name). She discovered that Bo had a good musical ear and saw to it that Bo learned how to play the violin, a training that in the end turned him into a fan of violin jazz, with Svend Asmussen and Stéphane Grappelli as his idols.

The hot fiddler in 1973. (Courtesy Anna Södersten Bengtsson)

A Lucky Boy

Bo was lucky, because unlike the other children in his family he was given the opportunity to study, something that he was enormously grateful for later in life. He always contended that "school grades are the best friends of the poor." Bo was conscious of the fact that he had been lucky. "I am a social climber, a satisfied social climber," he stated in an interview in 1991, "When I look back at my father's life in the mine, I feel terrified thinking that life could be like that."[3]

High school years. Standing, left to right: Bo, Stig, Helge, Erik. Sitting, left to right: Greta, Alice, Sigrid. (Courtesy Anna Södersten Bengtsson)

When the time came to begin high school, Bo had to move from Grängesberg to Ludvika. He stayed with the family of his classmate Gunnar Eriksson who would later become professor of the history of ideas at Uppsala—the beginning of a lifelong friendship. He graduated from high school in Ludvika in 1951, specializing in humanities and classics—Greek and Latin— with top marks.

---

[3] Söderberg (1991).

Top student 1951. (Courtesy Anna Södersten Bengtsson)

CHAPTER 2

Uppsala

After his military service, Bo began to study social sciences at Uppsala University in 1952, getting a bachelor's degree at the beginning of 1955 and, after spending the spring semester that year at L'École des Sciences Politiques in Paris, a Politices Magister degree at Uppsala the following year: political science, sociology, statistics, and economics. Thereafter he continued his studies in economics for the licentiate degree, with Erik Lindahl and Ragnar Bentzel as his supervisors, which he finished in 1959, after spending six months at the London School of Economics.

THE LICENTIATE THESIS

Bo Södersten's licentiate thesis dealt with the development of Sweden's foreign trade in a long-run perspective.[1] The first chapter, which occupies half the space, is devoted to a survey of the development of trade from 1870 until the beginning of the 1950s, divided into a number of shorter subperiods: 1870–1890, 1890–1913, 1921–1939, and 1946–1955 (omitting the two world wars). Bo shows how the composition of exports and imports changed during each of these periods. From 1870 to 1890, Sweden's foreign trade developed rapidly. The country became an

---

[1] Södersten (1959a).

increasingly open economy. Exports were dominated by raw materials: wood and iron, imports by food and textiles.

During the following period, the structure changed. The ratio of foreign trade to GDP decreased and the share of wood in exports was reduced while paper and pulp exports expanded. On the metal side a similar change took place. Iron and steel stagnated while the exports of engineering industry products increased considerably. The exports of iron ore increased as well, thanks to the Bessemer and Martin methods, which made it possible to use the phosphorous ores of the mining districts of central and northern Sweden. The imports of both food and textiles decreased while those of inputs for the Swedish manufacturing industry increased: ores and metals, coal and coke, as well chemical products.

The interwar years displayed a less clear-cut connection between foreign trade and national income than the previous two periods. Paper and pulp continued to be the most important export products, while the share of the wood industry decreased. Ores and engineering products expanded. After the end of the war, the trend toward autarky in food production continued and so did the increase of imports for the manufacturing sector. Engineering dominated the exports of the metal sector, but far more important were paper, pulp, and wood products.

The second chapter of the thesis deals with the development of Sweden's terms-of-trade between 1870 and 1955. Different definitions of the concept are discussed and thereafter Bo constructs his own model, with two completely specialized economies, of what determines the terms-of-trade.[2] The central variables, given zero growth in the trading partner countries, are the growth rate of GDP, the income elasticity of imports, and the demand elasticities of the country's exports and imports, respectively, with respect to the terms-of-trade. (If there is growth among the trading partners too, the development of the terms-of-trade will be influenced by the corresponding variables there as well.)

Bo tests his model on Swedish data, assuming that Sweden was able to influence its export prices. The "income elasticities" that he estimates are not the "usual" or theoretically correct *ceteris paribus* elasticities. That would be impossible. "It is certainly of interest, however, in the first stage of the analysis ... to determine the connection between national income

---

[2] The model was published in Södersten (1959b). His sources of inspiration were Hicks (1953) and Johnson (1955).

and the demand for imports during a given historical process."[3] Bo works with two different model formulations. In the first, the exterior world is assumed to be stationary, whereas in the second one a growth rate and an income elasticity of demand are assumed.

Bo was aware of the strong simplifications that he made, but still claimed that he had succeeded in arriving at a good fit to the historical data. "Summing up, it may be said that the approach applied ... has turned out to be fruitful. Since the model employed has been highly abstract and has worked with large aggregates it has not been possible to arrive at anything but a general picture of the factors determining the development."[4]

The third chapter of the licentiate thesis deals with the Swedish import capacity and balance of payments and the connection between the two. The import capacity (the income terms-of-trade) is defined as the value of exports divided by an index of the import prices, or, which amounts to the same thing, the commodity terms-of-trade (the export price index divided by the import price index) times the export volume. Bo opposed the idea that it was deteriorating terms-of-trade which caused balance of payments problems. It was not possible to disregard the influence of the export volume, which he could verify with Swedish data.

In the last chapter, Bo discusses the relative importance of the development of prices and productivity for the development of export shares in five export industries. He constructs a profitability index: the development of prices multiplied with the development of productivity. What mainly had driven the development was productivity changes. In the expanding branches productivity had increased continuously while contracting branches displayed stagnating or decreasing productivity. Bo thought that he could see a difference in the patterns which could explain that both expanding and contracting industries increased their profitability:

> Relatively speaking, the supply side must be regarded as the active side, the parameter side, of an industry. An industry can itself affect its supply actively while it can only indirectly affect its demand. It may hence be that the difference is that the expanding export branches themselves created the preconditions for an improvement of their profitability indices by applying productivity-increasing innovations. That stagnating industries also saw an improvement of their profitability indices was due to the fact that their

[3] Södersten (1959a), p. 74.
[4] Ibid., p. 80.

prices were brought up by a 'pull-effect' due to the general income increase resulting from the productivity increases in the expanding branches.[5]

The examiner of Bo's licentiate thesis was Ragnar Bentzel. He awarded him a *magna cum laude* both on the thesis and on the final examination.

INCIPIENT SOCIALIST AGITATOR

During his Uppsala years, Bo Södersten became a member of the Social Democratic student club Laboremus and also served as its president in 1956. This gave him a forum for spreading the ideas that he had imbibed at home and strengthened through his own reading of Socialist literature during his school years. Bo had a definite impact on his fellow students. The journalist Hans O. Sjöström was one of the young men who received their first insights into the virtues of Socialism through their membership in Laboremus. He is eight years younger than Bo Södersten and has testified as to the electrifying effect that Bo's writings, speeches, and interventions during the discussions in the club had on his contemporaries. In 1960, Bo published an article on Socialism in the Social Democratic journal *Tiden*, where he argued that it was impossible to arrive at equality in a society with private property:[6]

> For some of us, Södersten's article about socialization acquired an importance which reminded of the one which Mao's little red book got for a younger generation of Laboremites. Södersten's thoughts about socialization as a means for equality [were clearly presented]. Thereby, the text got a much stronger propagandistic impact and served as a source of inspiration both for new recruits and older ones who thought that the eternal grinding of stencils in the Community Center [Folkets Hus] was not always meaningful.[7]

---

[5] Ibid., pp. 106–07.
[6] Södersten (1960), reprinted in Södersten (1968b).
[7] Sjöström (1987), p. 82.

Still agitator: Bo in the 1980s. (Courtesy Anna Södersten Bengtsson)

Not only that. Sjöström argues that Bo was a model in other ways as well. "He had a heretic attitude towards life and politics. He liked to resort to religious parables when he wrote about political and economic issues." In an article in *Libertas*, the ideological journal of the Swedish Social Democratic Student Association, called "Paulus och den fria konkurrensen [Paul and Free Competition]," he contended that "The acceptance of competition by the Socialists has been ... problematic and painful. It has reminded of the attitude of Paul toward intimate intercourse: it had better not take place and if it does take place, you should at any rate not enjoy it."[8] This, states Sjöström, was more than a way of writing: it was an

[8] Södersten (1959c), p. 7.

attitude, a way of exposing ridiculous standpoints by pushing them into the absurd. He ridiculed the Socialist stance: "We seem to be in the same predicament as Jesus, when he was tempted by the Devil: if we only abjure our faith [in free competition] the riches of the world will be at our feet."[9] Sjöström rightfully points out that Bo's attitude displayed a great deal of arrogance toward those who did not share his views. They were simply displaying confused beliefs. This, as we will have several occasions to observe in the following, was an attitude that would frequently come to the surface.

With his family in the 1950s. From left to right: Greta, Wiktor, Anna, Bo. (Courtesy Birgit Friggebo)

Bo was capable of inspiring other people not only ideologically. Nils Lundgren has testified how, at the beginning of the 1960s, when he worked as an assistant to Bo, analytical discussions of politics and literature with him contributed to the creation of an intellectual attitude to life, in

---

[9] Ibid.

general, and to social issues, in particular.[10] It is easy to understand, because when Bo moved away from the charged ideological field, relaxed and offered samples of his cultural erudition, he was at his very best.

Literary Interlude

Bo Södersten also had a literary vein, which he let flow during his Uppsala years in two contexts, both of which to a large extent appear to be autobiographic. The novel *Kandidaterna* (*The Students*) was never published.[11] It was probably refused. No wonder. Both the intrigue and the portraits of the people feel stereotype. The plot centers on the courtship of the protagonist, Harry Ramberg, of a girl, which comes to an abrupt end as he leaves her. This is interspersed with academic lecture and seminar scenes, quasi-philosophical late evening discussions, the need for a "hero of our time" and, of course, politics, mainly within the frame of the Social Democratic student club, Laboremus, and sundry intimate scenes, The women bulge in front and the skirts are inevitably tight on the rear end. "Have you ever met a woman who has been intellectually stimulating?" asks Harry.[12]

Bo in his late twenties. (Courtesy Birgit Friggebo)

[10] Lundgren (2011).
[11] Södersten (n.d.).
[12] Ibid., p. 50.

In 1962, Bo published a collection of short stories, *Övertygelser* (*Convictions*),[13] a title which in all probability had been inspired by the English collection of essays, *Conviction*, written by a number of young Socialists.[14] It did not turn out too well, he writes, in his unpublished and unfinished draft of memoirs:

> My collection of short stories—if not plagiarized—at least was inspired by 'Dubliners' by James Joyce.[15] One of my thoughts was that the stories should not make any point—at least no clear point. (Roughly as in Joyce.) The book ... fell flat. There is not too much to be said about that.[16]

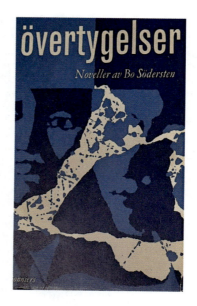

Short stories

---

[13] Södersten (1962a).

[14] MacKenzie (1958). The party was impressive: Norman MacKenzie, Peter Shore, Brian Abel-Smith, Raymond Williams, Peter Townsend, Richard Hoggart, Nigel Calder, Hugh Thomas, Peter Marris, Mervyn Jones, Paul Johnson and Iris Murdoch.

[15] Joyce (1914).

[16] Södersten (2001a).

Hans O. Sjöström read the stories: "The attempt can hardly be classified as successful. The stories are written in protest against the common opinion that short stories should contain some kind of point. Södersten's stories hence lack points, but do not contain any substitute for what has been lost."[17] It is obvious that the stories are partly autobiographical, above all the title story, "Övertygelser," which deals with the conflict between a traditional Social Democratic trade unionist father and his rebellious son—a frustrated academic—who attempts to teach him what Socialism is while at the same time he is planning to seduce an upper-class girl and turn her into a Socialist. The young man cannot stand the slow pace of everyday Socialism. He wants to give his life for the Party, but the Party refuses his sacrifice.

You cannot but agree both with the author and with Sjöström. The book is not good. The seven stories, with a single exception, deal with some kind of love. The blurb of the book summarizes:

> Love—and its company—jealousy, betrayal and the secret, perhaps unconscious reservations—is the constant theme of the collection of short stories that marks the debut of Bo Södersten. In different ways and phases this love is portrayed: as young love and deep devotion but also as somewhat shabbily practiced sex.

---

[17] Sjöström (1987), p. 84.

CHAPTER 3

Doctor

After his licentiate thesis, Bo continued toward his doctoral degree at Stockholm University, with Ingvar Svennilson as his supervisor. He was an assistant teacher there between 1960–1961 and 1963–1964. From September 1961 to December 1962, he was in the United States, at MIT in Cambridge and the University of California, Berkeley. He then got in touch with Richard Caves, Harry Johnson, Dale Jorgenson, Charles Kindleberger, and Tibor Scitovsky, who read some of the early drafts of his dissertation. Bo continued on the track from the licentiate thesis: international trade and economic growth, but the doctoral dissertation was completely theoretical and mathematical.

Before that, he extended the theoretical analysis of his licentiate thesis in an article in *Ekonomisk Tidskrift*, 1961.[1] There, he worked with two countries, both producing and consuming two goods. Production is determined by a time trend (growth) and by the relative price of the two goods (the terms-of-trade) and consumption by the national incomes of the two countries and the relative prices. With the aid of this model, Bo determines the change in the terms-of-trade. The article also discusses the applicability of the model to the question of the development of the terms-of-trade between developed and developing countries

---

[1] Södersten (1961), English translation: Södersten (1962b).

© The Author(s), under exclusive license to Springer Nature Switzerland AG 2022
M. Lundahl, *Bo Södersten from Left to Right*, Palgrave Studies in the History of Economic Thought,
https://doi.org/10.1007/978-3-031-09101-8_3

Bo's analysis of the balance of trade and the terms-of-trade also constitutes the background to an article from 1962, on "the new dollar crisis."[2] At the end of the 1940s and the beginning of the 1950s, Europe had experienced a shortage of dollars, due to a large surplus on the American current account of the balance of payments. It was only because of the large contributions of the United States to other Western countries that the latter had access to dollars, through the resulting deficit of the American balance of payments. At the end of the 1950s, this had reached the highest level of the decade. At the same time, the American gold reserve had shrunk, which might become a problem should foreign dollar holders insist on converting dollars to gold.

Bo attempted to find out which the reasons for the increasing deficit might be. Inflation was no higher in the United States than in other OEEC countries and an application of the kind of two-sector models he had used himself yielded no clear-cut conclusions, because they were difficult to quantify. Explanations in terms of loss of comparative advantage in research and development and the U.S. foreign aid proved inconclusive as well. In the end, hence, it was difficult to formulate remedies.

The Doctoral Dissertation: Growth and Trade

Bo Södersten's doctoral dissertation forms part of the neoclassical tradition of foreign trade which goes back to Eli Heckscher and Bertil Ohlin[3] and which by John Hicks, Tadeusz Rybczynski, Harry Johnson, and Ronald Findlay and Harry Grubert had been extended to the comparative static investigation of how economic growth (of GDP) affected the terms-of-trade, production, and the national income.[4]

Hicks, on the occasion of his inaugural lecture as Drummond Professor of Political Economy at Oxford, in 1953, after paying due homage to all his predecessors, dissected the effects of differences in productivity increases in two countries trading with each other, in a hard to follow verbal analysis, where he introduced the notions of export and import biased growth, depending on in which sector of the economy the

---

[2] Södersten (1962c).
[3] Heckscher (1919), English translation, Heckscher (1991), Ohlin (1922), English translation, Ohlin (2002), Ohlin (1924), English translation: Ohlin (1991), Ohlin (1933).
[4] Hicks (1953), Rybczynski (1955), Johnson (1955), Findlay and Grubert (1959).

productivity increase takes place.[5] Rybczynski, in turn, complemented the three main neoclassical trade theorems—Heckscher-Ohlin, factor price equalization, and Stolper-Samuelson on tariffs—with the fourth cornerstone: the effects of factor growth on production in the two-goods setting, one of the most simple and most useful theorems in international economics.[6]

Following Hicks and Rybczynski, Harry Johnson provided a mixed verbal and mathematical (footnotes) analysis of the effects of growth on the volume of trade and the terms-of-trade between an industrial Mancumia and an agrarian Agraria, distinguishing not only between the causes of economic expansion but also between pro-trade and anti-trade bias in the latter country due to the sectoral origin of the production increases.[7] The last building block for Bo's dissertation was provided by a paper written by two young MIT graduate students, Ronald Findlay and Harry Grubert, dealing with the effects of differently biased technical progress on the terms-of-trade.[8]

In his dissertation, Bo works within the standard 2×2×2 framework of two countries, two production factors and two goods.[9] In the basic model, the sources of growth are not specified. As time goes by, the production capacity of the two countries simply increases. Bo demonstrates that the sectoral origin of growth is of fundamental importance for the development of relative prices and the national income. If growth is concentrated to the import-competing sector in Country 1, an improvement of the terms-of-trade will reinforce the effect of growth on the national income. (So will growth in the export sector of Country 2.) A strong growth of the demand for the export good of Country 1 works in the same direction. Growth in the export sector of Country 1 (and in the import sector of Country 2) may, on the other hand, lead to deteriorating terms-of-trade which will counteract the direct growth effect. The ability to adjust production when prices change will play an important role for the end result.[10] This is formally expressed through the demand and supply elasticities in

---

[5] Hicks (1953).
[6] Rybczynski (1955).
[7] Johnson (1955).
[8] Findlay and Grubert (1959).
[9] Södersten (1964a).
[10] Bo also investigates which conditions must be met for a country to 'export away' its growth, i.e. the case when ahe deterioration of the terms-of-trade is so large that the terms-of-trade deteriorate so much that the national income is reduced ('impoverishing growth').

the denominator of the expression for the change of the terms-of-trade. (Analysis of the denominator—the "elasticity factor"—was a recurrent ingredient in Bo's exams for the last-year undergraduate students of international economics.)

In the next step, growth is specified as factor accumulation (labor and capital). The Rybczynski theorem tells us that, with linearly homogeneous production functions, when one factor grows while the other one remains constant, the production of the good using the growing factor intensively will increase, while the production of the other good will decrease.[11] Rybczynski also deduced the effects on relative prices. His analysis was geometric. Bo demonstrates mathematically which factors on the production and consumption side determine the result. He also shows what happens to the national income.[12]

Bo also deals with the case where growth is caused by technical progress, represented by a parameter, t, in the production functions of the two goods.[13] The results are those expected. What happens depends, on the one hand, on whether technical change is neutral—increasing the marginal productivities of the production factors in the same proportion—or they increase that of one of the factors more than that of the other, and, on the other hand, on in which sector they take place. To this you have to add the effects of the changes on the demand side induced by growth.[14]

The penultimate chapter of the dissertation is devoted to the special case when the factor proportions used in the production of the two goods cannot be varied—an excursus, as Bo himself refers to it. He begins by analyzing growth (specified as capital accumulation) in a closed economy, before he introduces international trade into the model. The second part of the chapter discusses what happens when growth occurs in an economy with an infinitely elastic supply of labor, that is, an economy where labor is available at a given wage rate.[15] Growth is generated through capital accumulation in the "modern" sector, which when it grows may employ labor from the "traditional" sector, "agriculture." The national income increases,

---

[11] Rybczynski (1955).

[12] Bo also provides expressions for the development of factor prices. Unfortunately, when deriving them, he used expressions assuming given commodity prices (Södersten 1964a, pp. 81–84), which was observed in a critical review by Johansson and Jungenfelt (1964).

[13] His analysis develops that of Findlay och Grubert (1959).

[14] Again, the results with respect to the development of factor prices (Södersten 1964a, pp. 112–14) are derived on the erroneous assumption of given relative commodity prices.

[15] Cf. Lewis (1954).

which in turn leads to changes on the demand side. Technical progress too will generate increased employment in the modern sector, unless it is labor-saving.[16]

Bo rounds up his dissertation with a discussion of how growth and the terms-of-trade have been dealt with in the economic literature over time. The discussion concentrates on two distinct "schools": the "English" one and the one mainly associated with Hans Singer and Raúl Prebisch, which contends that there is a tendency for the terms-of-trade of raw material producing developing countries to deteriorate over time. The two schools are very much each other's opposites. The former goes back to Robert Torrens' *An Essay on the Production of Wealth* from 1821[17] and continues up to Keynes[18] and other modern economists. The main message of the English school was that the terms-of-trade of countries exporting industrial products were deteriorating because of diminishing returns in countries exporting agricultural products pushed up the price of agricultural goods.

The Singer-Prebisch hypothesis in turn is based on the assumption that the income elasticity of demand for industrial goods is higher than the one for raw materials and on the low flexibility of production of the economies of the developing countries which made it difficult for them to switch from one product to another when relative prices changed. To this were added arguments about asymmetric development of price across the trade cycle, monopolistic markets in developed countries and competitive markets in developing economies, strong trade unions in the former and weak ones in the latter.[19] Bo contended that these hypotheses are so vaguely formulated that they cannot be converted into any consistent model and instead holds out the elasticity hypothesis as the central element of the Singer-Prebisch thesis, a hypothesis which may at least be discussed with the aid of the model that he uses himself in his dissertation.

Bo Södersten defended his thesis on 15 May 1964, with Tore Thonstad from Oslo as his first opponent and Erling Olsen from Copenhagen as his

---

[16] In 1981, Bo came back to a model which partly built on the Lewis approach, in a comment to a paper by Ronald Findlay (1981), (Södersten 1981b), which rested on as combination of Robert Solow's (1956) growth model and Lewis' (1969) model of the terms-of-trade, the former applied to industrial and the latter to developing countries.

[17] Torrens (1821).

[18] Keynes (1912).

[19] Singer (1950), Prebisch (1950).

second opponent. His defense was one of the longest on record. In order to understand why, it is necessary to make a detour.

Housing Policy: The Three Rents

In 1963, Bo began a polemic which led to a very long animosity between him and Assar Lindbeck. In an essay with the title "Bostadsbristen och de tre räntorna (The Housing Shortage and the Three Rents)," he reviewed Ragnar Bentzel's, Lindbeck's, and Ingemar Ståhl's *Bostadsbristen: En studie av prisbildningen på bostadsmarknaden* (*The Housing Shortage: A Study of Price Formation in the Housing Market*),[20] where the three authors advocated deregulation and market pricing.[21] Bo insinuated that they had not been motivated simply by scientific devotion but that political value judgments which they had not accounted for were behind their work. His thesis was that the three did not take into account that housing was not a simple consumer durable but had an extreme life span which was difficult to grasp and which might make for underinvestment. The market mechanism did not provide correct information.

Housing also yielded three "rents" which accrued to the homeowners. The first one was a Ricardian rent. As construction expanded outward, away from the city centers, prices in the more attractive locations increased. The second rent was due to inflation. The rents paid by the tenants increased in terms of current prices while the cost of the capital which the owners had borrowed remained fixed. This led to a transfer of income and wealth to the latter. The third rent was due to the fact that productivity development had been slower in the construction industry than elsewhere which made the price not only of newly produced houses but also of already existing dwellings increase in relation to other prices.

The Thesis Defense

Assar Lindbeck never forgot the review and took revenge on a number of occasions. The first was Bo's thesis defense. He attempted to persuade Bo's supervisor, Ingvar Svennilson, not to allow the dissertation to be defended. Lindbeck had set up a PM with no less than forty-nine strongly critical points which he distributed to Svennilson and Anders Östlind.

---

[20] Bentzel et al. (1963).
[21] Södersten (1963), reprinted in Södersten (1968b).

Lindbeck had found "a large number of mistakes, partly serious" which he shared.[22] Svennilson, however, refused and told Lindbeck that none of his points would be considered unless he stated them in public. The defense dragged on for several hours. After the two official opponents came the opponents *ex auditorio*. Gunnar Myrdal, who was in the middle of his most institutional period ever, busy with his work on *Asian Drama*,[23] complained about Bo's "high school mathematics" and about the use of formal models in general. Assar Lindbeck was extremely harsh. "He was so mad that he was about to explode," remembers Bo's old school mate Gunnar Eriksson.[24] Lindbeck was followed by Karl Jungenfelt and Östen Johansson who had found a formal mistake in the derivation of some formulas. In the end, it became so late that the defense almost interfered with the traditional post-defense dinner.

The thesis committee met eleven days after the defense. It consisted of five economists: professors Gunnar Myrdal, Erik Lundberg, Ingvar Svennilson, and Anders Östlind; and acting professor Assar Lindbeck; plus the professor of geography David Hannerberg and the professor of theoretical philosophy Anders Wedberg. Tore Thonstad had sent a summary of his opposition. Bo had used asymmetrical definitions of the shifts in the production possibility curves for the two goods in the model. His interpretation of the derived formulas left a lot to be desired. Partly they were erroneous and some of the results which appeared to be novel had been derived from false premises. According to Thonstad, the most original part of the dissertation was the one dealing with technical progress. Bo was awarded a *cum laude* but without qualifying for the degree of *docent* (the equivalent of associate professor), the degree which would open the door to a future academic career.

Östen Johansson och Karl Jungenfelt published their opposition in *Ekonomisk Tidskrift*.[25] They claimed that the unspecified growth model was an unnecessary complication. It would have been better to analyze factor accumulation and technical progress directly. Johansson and Jungenfelt also took issue with the failure to include savings in the model. There was not much that found grace before the eyes of the harsh judges. The use of comparative statics was a weakness. The conclusions were trivial but simultaneously complicated and obscure. The assumptions were too restrictive, to the

[22] Lindbeck (1969b).
[23] Myrdal (1968).
[24] Interview with Gunnar Eriksson, 14 April 2021.
[25] Johansson och Jungenfelt (1964).

point where they spoiled the explanatory value of the model. The economic interpretation of the results was incorrect in some instances. It was not possible to draw dynamic conclusions from a comparative static model. The account of the derivation of the formulas was incomplete and sometimes outrightly erroneous. The model could not be used for the analysis of trade between developed and developing countries.[26]

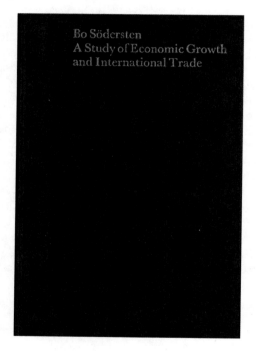

Bad or good?

Other reviewers were more positive. Murray Kemp wrote briefly in *American Economic Review* that Bo had provided "a well-nigh complete compendium of answers" to "a clearly defined class of comparative statical exercises," that his discussion of the effects of growth when factor proportions are fixed constituted "a bonus" and that his dissection of Raúl Prebisch was "crushing." Kemp's conclusion was that Bo's work had been well worth the

---

[26] Bo answered his critics (Södersten, 1964b).

effort and that he had done it well, with as gracious a style as the subject permitted.[27] Egon Neuberger published a more detailed scrutiny in *Kyklos*.[28] He called the book "an impressive example of successful model building for the purpose of examining rigorously some extremely complex issues of theory and policy,"[29] referred to Bo as a highly competent theorist and concluded that the dissertation was an excellent contribution to the theory of international trade.

In the *Economic Journal*, Athanasios Asimakopoulos wrote that Bo's book constituted the definitive, exhausting treatment of the 2×2×2 model of international trade when the changes in the production functions are exogenous. The expressions derived were frequently complex, but they were arranged in a way which made them easy to interpret. The production functions employed were not necessarily linearly homogeneous, but in order to arrive at clear-cut results Bo had to revert to this more restrictive formulation. Asimakopoulos also pointed to the principal difficulties deriving from the assumption that the capital stock could increase without any saving. Altogether, however, he thought that the book was well-written and of interest to everybody working on international trade.[30]

* * *

The mid-1960s were a difficult period for Bo. He felt frustrated—for several reasons. Hans O. Sjöström remembers:

> The doctoral dissertation had had a cold reception, and so had the short stories. He felt misunderstood and isolated. The road to a professorship appeared to be a long one. It was from that position that he had planned to build a platform as an influential social debater.
> – But, said Södersten when we met at the local Stockholm chapter of the Social Democratic party in 1964, Strindberg was also misunderstood.
> He also said that if we would get power and influence, we should not pull any punches. The party needed purge and renewal.[31]

---

[27] Kemp (1964).
[28] Neuberger (1965).
[29] Ibid., p. 389.
[30] Asimakopoulos (1966).
[31] Sjöström (1987), p. 85.

CHAPTER 4

After the Dissertation

When Bo Södersten had defended his dissertation, he substituted for Torsten Gårdlund as acting professor of international economics at Lund University in 1964–1965. Gårdlund was in Tunisia working for the Ford Foundation as economic advisor in the Ministry of Finance. Thereafter, Bo followed Horace Greeley's advice and went west. During 1965–1966 and 1966–1967, he was visiting lecturer at the University of California, Berkeley. There, he began working on a modern textbook in international economics, and there he also met the Danish mathematical economist Karl Vind. In March 1966, Bo Södersten was finally awarded the title of *docent* of international economics in Lund. In April, he got a lectureship in economics and the following year an associate professorship in international economics.

Articles

At the same time as he worked on his textbook, Bo followed up his dissertation with a couple of technical articles. The first was written with Karl-Göran Mäler.[1] The article compares John Hicks' and Murray Kemp's definitions of non-neutral technical progress, that is, technical progress that does not increase the marginal productivities of the production

[1] Mäler and Södersten (1967).

factors in the same proportion. The definitions were not equivalent and the impact of technical progress on the marginal rate of substitution between the production factors hence differs as well.

The second article, written with Karl Vind, was published in what latter-day economists obsessed with rankings have classified as the leading economics journal in the world, the *American Economic Review*.[2] It deals with the effects of a tariff on the national income and the terms-of-trade in two countries which trade with each other. The article contained a controversial result. Lloyd Metzler had in two papers questioned a result from the classic Stolper-Samuelson analysis: that a tariff increases the price on the imported good in the importing country.[3] His argument was that a tariff could induce an improvement of the terms-of-trade which was large enough to swamp the price-increasing effect of the tariff. Bo and Vind, however, argued that Metzler's result was due to the assumption that tariff revenues were spent in a way that differed from that of other incomes and that hence the Stolper-Samuelson analysis was valid.

Bo's and Vind's results were questioned by one of the leading international trade theorists of the time,[4] Ronald Jones, who, on the one hand, thought that their analysis was unnecessarily complicated and, on the other hand, demonstrated that the result was critically dependent on the assumption that the two goods were gross substitutes, that is, that in the two-good case, if the price of one of the goods increases, the demand for the other good will always increase. A price increase, however, has two effects: a substitution effect—the demand for the goods whose price does not increase tends to grow—and an income effect—an increase of the price of the good represents a decrease of the income of the consumer—which tends to reduce the price of both goods. The income effect is negative and may be stronger than the substitution effect for the good in question. Södersten and Vind had, however, simply assumed that this case could not arise, a fatal error, according to Jones.

Bo and Vind defended themselves. An assumption can never be right or wrong. To argue otherwise was nonsense. And their problem formulation was based on more fundamental concepts (production and consumption) than that of Jones (offer curves—a derived concept), and hence richer in content and easier to interpret than his.[5]

---

[2] Södersten and Vind (1968).
[3] Stolper and Samuelson (1941), Metzler (1949a, 1949b).
[4] Jones (1969).
[5] Södersten and Vind (1969).

LATER EFFORTS

Bo came back to international economic themes also in later years, but not in any systematic fashion. They figured among his many newspaper articles (see below), often topics related to the contemporary political and economic situation, and also in anthologies that he edited, including the EEC-EC-EU question, notably the issue of Swedish entry and the effects on the Swedish economy, the EMU, exchange rate issues (fixed vs flexible exchange rates), protectionism, developments in international economics during the post-war period, immigration (to Sweden).

Bo's last journal article on an international subject, from 2002, is co-authored with Karolina Ekholm.[6] There he goes back to the theme of economic growth and international trade, but the causal order is reversed. Which is the effect of international trade on economic growth? This was a field which had not been treated as analytically rigorously as the effects of growth on trade. Karolina's and Bo's article attempted to do precisely that. Their point of departure was the income terms-of-trade: export prices divided by import prices, that is, the commodity terms-of-trade, multiplied by the export volume—a measure of the import capacity of a country. The hypothesis was that fast-growing countries displayed rapidly increasing income terms-of-trade. It was tested on five fast-growing Asian countries—Hong Kong, Japan, South Korea, Malaysia, and Singapore—and five old industrial countries—Austria, France, Sweden, Great Britain, and the United States.

Data from 1970 to 1995 indicated that the income terms-of-trade both for the fast-growing Asian countries and the more slowly growing Western economies increased faster than their GDP per capita. The former had managed to expand their exports without running into deteriorating relative prices, which Karolina and Bo interpreted as a successful diversification of exports into sectors with high income elasticities of demand or of increased quality of exports. They had also profited from the increased integration of the international economy.

---

[6] Ekholm and Södersten (2002).

Bo around 1969. (Courtesy Birgit Friggebo)

THE GUY WITH THE BOOK

In 1969 it was ready: the Book—the one that Bo had begun working on in Berkeley in 1965–1966 and which he himself regarded as his best work. In international circles, he became known as "the Guy with the Book." The book was *International Economics*, and it was the first textbook in international economics which built on consistent application of general equilibrium theory. It was published in Swedish in 1969,[7] and the following year in English.[8] Those of us who were his undergraduate students in international economics in Lund got it first in mimeographed form, chapter by chapter, from a teacher sprouting enthusiasm during his entire lecture series, and the book was not ready when the course was over.

When the book had been finished, it consisted of five sections. The first one presents the traditional static theory of international trade: Ricardo and the gains from trade, comparative advantage in the Heckscher-Ohlin formulation, the factor price equalization theorem, the effects of trade on the income distribution, and the Leontief paradox—the United States, a country abundantly endowed with capital, was found to export labor-intensive commodities.

The second part builds on Bo's dissertation. He begins with a pedagogical historical account of international trade and economic growth during the nineteenth and twentieth centuries, before he presents the different chapters of his dissertation: the effects of unspecified growth, the Rybczynski theorem, and the effects of different kinds of technical progress. Bo finishes

---

[7] Södersten (1969a).
[8] Södersten (1970a).

with a discussion of the effects of growth on the terms-of-trade as exposed by the classical English school and Singer-Prebisch.

The book

In the third part of the book, Bo goes into the macroeconomic aspects of international economics: the balance of payments. He deals with national accounting and the composition of the national income in an open economy, the connection between the national income and the balance of payments, the international propagation of business cycles, the functioning of the international currency market, and the advantages and disadvantages of fixed and flexible exchange rates. Finally, he discusses how external and internal equilibrium can be achieved simultaneously: equilibrium in the balance of payments and full employment.

The fourth part of *International Economics* deals with international trade policy: the effects of tariffs under optimal market conditions, the optimal tariff for a country which is large enough to be able to influence world market prices, quantitative import restrictions, tariffs, and subsidies when distortions are present in the commodity or factor markets, effective or implicit tariffs (tariffs on value added). Two chapters are more empirical and institutional. The first one deals with the GATT, the EEC, and the tariff reduction proposals within the so-called Kennedy Round and the second one with UNCTAD and trade preferences for less developed countries and with stabilization of international raw material prices. The theory of customs unions is presented, as well as the classical transfer problem: the effects on the balance of payments of a capital transfer from one country to another. Finally, the theory of direct investment and the effects of the latter on the investing and host counties is discussed.

The last section of *International Economics* examines the international payment system. It begins with a presentation of the problem of international liquidity taking the U.S. balance of payments and the balance between gold and dollar holdings in the currency reserve as its point of departure. The role of the IMF is highlighted. The next chapter discusses the adequacy of international liquidity, the price of liquidity, the American seigniorage from providing dollars, and the adjustment mechanism of the international payment system when a country runs into a deficit in its balance of payments. The last chapter of the book presents the different plans for reform of the international payments system that were discussed around 1970.

CRITICISM AND COMPETITION

Bertil Ohlin reviewed the Swedish edition of *International Economics*.[9] He pointed out that the book could serve as an intermediate level university text, but the need for a book in Swedish was not pressing. Students at that level could easily read articles in English. The review was mainly critical. Ohlin insinuated that Bo had not understood the importance of demand factors when it came to the establishment of international trade patterns, that the discussion of growth and trade failed to deal with the impact of trade on the factor supply, and that social factors, such as legislation and taxation, were absent from the discussion. He ended with a personal twist: "The original contributions of the author are neither numerous nor important, but providing that is hardly the purpose of a textbook."[10]

Bo answered Ohlin's criticism.[11] He had indeed paid attention to demand factors, stressing the general equilibrium nature of international trade theory, not least in his presentation of the Heckscher-Ohlin

[9] Ohlin (1969a).
[10] Ibid.
[11] Södersten (1969b).

theorem. Either Ohlin had not read his book carefully enough or—sensationally—had not understood the implications of the model connected with his own name. Bo quoted a recent survey of international trade theory by John Chipman, who stated that "it became evident that Heckscher himself had forthrightly stated the [factor prize equalization] theorem in terms of complete equalization, and that Ohlin's many qualifications had tended to obscure the underlying logic."[12] In other words, Bo contended, Ohlin simply screwed up what Heckscher had originated. Ohlin answered, repeating his criticism and adding that Bo had not paid any attention to the influence of transport costs in his book.[13]

In spite of Ohlin's criticism, *International Economics* was a commercial success. It was translated into Italian, Portuguese, and Hungarian.[14] For a few years, it was alone of its kind in the international textbook market. A second Swedish edition was published,[15] and two English ones,[16] updated as the institutions of the international economy changed, and new theories saw the daylight. This is true not least for the third English edition, where Geoffrey Reed from Nottingham University had become co-author. There, the theory of intra-industrial trade and international trade under conditions of imperfect competition is given a prominent position and so is the trade policy choice of developing countries: import substitution or export promotion. International factor mobility has been included as well as the political economy of protectionism. On the macro side it was inevitable that flexible exchange rates had to be stressed, something which hardly existed when the first edition was published. The updates were necessary, not only because of the theoretical developments. The first edition of Richard Caves' and Ronald Jones' *World Trade and Payments* was published in 1973[17] and Paul Krugman's and Maurice Obstfeld's

---

[12] Chipman (1966), p. 19.
[13] Ohlin (1969b).
[14] Södersten (1976a, 1979a, 1985a). In addition, an Indian economist attempted to publish large parts of Bo's text as his own—a case of blatant plagiarism.
[15] Södersten (1978a).
[16] Södersten (1980a), Södersten and Reed (1994).
[17] Caves and Jones (1973).

International Economics: Theory and Policy in 1987,[18] books that with time would become too powerful competitors. Bo's book, however, tagged along for more than twenty-five years: no mean feat.[19]

---

[18] Krugman och Obstfeld (1987).
[19] In 1971, *International Economics* got a sequel: *Internationella resursfördelningsproblem* (*Problems of International Resource Allocation*), an elementary textbook which formed part of an experimental television and radio course in economics, in five parts, one of which was international economics. The book was written by Bo and his assistant at the time, Inga Persson (Persson and Södersten 1971).

CHAPTER 5

Essays

Between 1959 and 1961, Bo was a member of the editorial board of the Social Democratic journal *Tiden*. This provided an opportunity for him to cultivate a genre which attracted him a lot: the essay, including book reviews, a genre which did justice to his stylistic ability. In 1968, he published the first of four collections of essays: *Den hierarkiska välfärden* (*The Hierarchic Welfare*),[1] articles published mainly in *Tiden* between 1959 and 1968, inspired—exactly like the collection of short stories—by the democratic, reformist, English Socialists in *Conviction*—a series of essays which rest on a strong ideological foundation.

Economic and Politics

The first part deals with economics and politics.[2] There, Bo takes issue with John Kenneth Galbraith's thesis in *The Affluent Society*[3] that consumption has reached the stage where the consumers are satiated. Bo did not agree, especially not when it came to new commodities. Nevertheless, the affluent society was about to be established and this called for a political distribution of consumption in a way which made for a genuinely

[1] Södersten (1968b).
[2] Bo's review of the book by Bentzel, Lindbeck, and Ståhl is reprinted there.
[3] Galbraith (1958).

The right color for the cover

better society. The only party which could accomplish that was the Social Democrats, but it could not be taken for granted.

> Only if the Social Democracy attempts to realize the dream of a new community spirit and a richer life which has always existed as an undercurrent within the movement will it be able to avoid the stagnation of affluence. Now, that the problems of poverty have soon been solved, the time has come to begin to realize the classless society.[4]

Sweden was still a class society with an extremely unequal distribution of wealth. It was not possible to realize socialist ideals in a society dominated by private capitalism, and marginal measures—social engineering—would soon be neutralized in such a society. A frontal attack was necessary. What the movement needed was not contentment but tireless efforts.

---

[4] Södersten (1968b), p. 18, first published as Södersten (1960).

In 1967, Galbraith published a new book, *The New Industrial State*,[5] where he claimed that the modern industrial society required planning, however, not by the state but by the large corporations which were technically advanced and could dictate prices. Bo thought that the idea was superficial. Technical progress could make entire branches obsolete. He also opposed Galbraith's thesis that the managers had taken over the decision making from the owners. A few families dominated the Swedish economy, and the group of technocrats that was being constituted had interests which coincided with those of the traditional owners.

A number of chapters in *Den hierarkiska välfärden* deal with planning and Socialism. The grip on the future of the Social Democrats was insufficient. A "searching" planning was required, manifested by increasingly political appointments in the ministries which based on scientific principles tackled the social issues and the long-term economic planning. Bo returned to the planning theme on several occasions. He doubted that it was possible to carry out rational planning in a capitalist economy. At some point, a choice had to made between a Liberal and a Socialist system. Bo wanted structural planning which could guarantee long-run economic growth. The market system could not handle externalities, increasing returns to scale and indivisibilities, but the state had to step in and steer the structural change.

In 1960, a commission was working on a new party program for the Social Democrats. The formulations employed suggested that the old demand for socialization was being watered down. Bo thought that the debate had ended on a side-track where thesis-chewing Marxists with ready-made solutions were facing revisionists whose only interest was efficiency. Socialization would not accomplish the latter, but it could indeed further equality and contribute to the creation of a class-less society. This, however, would make it easier to reconcile the latter goals with growth— something that you could not expect from capitalism. The party program did not offer anything novel but essentially consisted in variations on an already existing theme: the extension of the social and labor market policy. It beat around the bush when it came to the fundamental organization of the economy. Reforming the capitalist system in the direction of increased equality was not possible. Planning was necessary since the free market did not work in this respect. A powerful reform policy must rest on control of the income formation process.

[5] Galbraith (1967).

Bo was also interested in international Socialism, and in *Den hierarkiska välfärden* he writes about the Socialist International, a movement which in his view had not been overly successful. During the post-war years it had not had any political importance whatsoever. Bo traced its failure to the history of the International, above all the failure to share experiences during the inter-war years—notably between England and France. He argued that the international work on reform policies had to take goals like equality, the open society, and a richer cultural life as its points of departure. The main tools of the reform policy should be a planned economy and socialization. The state had to assume the responsibility for full employment. The influence of the capitalists had to be eroded and fenced in, and you should never take any steps back from a won position. The Socialist International had to deal with the fundamental questions.[6]

Herbert Tingsten

The second part of *Den hierarkiska välfärden* deals with journeys. We will come back to it below in the context of economic development. The third and last part consists of book reviews. The one which stands out deals with Herbert Tingsten's four-volume autobiography *Mitt liv* (*My Life*).[7] Tingsten was a legendary professor of political science in Stockholm, frequently the antagonist of Gunnar Myrdal, a Social Democrat who turned Liberal, the chief editor of *Dagens Nyheter*, the largest Swedish daily for a decade, a person always in the middle of the Swedish debate.

Bo deals with all four volumes of Tingsten's memoirs. Tingsten was never formally engaged in party politics but always represented himself. His life was marked by a contrast between nihilism and vitality which was difficult to explain in spite of the openness of his memoirs. Bo praised Tingsten because he was not self-righteous but wanted to provide a calm overview of his life. He was, however, not in any way beyond reproach.

---

[6] In his book of essays, Bo also included a review of James Meade's *Efficiency, Equality and the Ownership of Property* (Meade, 1964), which advocated increased taxation of incomes, wealth and realized capital gains, as well as education, as means for increasing equality. Bo doubted that this was enough and advocated socialization. Only when state ownership has been secured you can allow the price mechanism to function.

[7] Tingsten (1961, 1962, 1963, 1964).

Tingsten did not hesitate to assume positions which upset the owners of *Dagens Nyheter* during his years as chief editor, between 1946 and 1959, in sensitive questions like Swedish NATO membership, nuclear weapons, socialization, monarchy and state church until in 1959, he deserted the Liberal camp and argued in favor of the Social Democratic stance on pensions.

Tingsten had been a Social Democrat until 1944, and Bo perceived that in his later years he campaigned vehemently against his former party:

> When you look back on Tingsten's contributions to domestic policy ... it is difficult to find ... anything but a simple mimicker of bourgeois prejudices. His virtually complete lack of interest in economic issues and his disgust of politics in its result-chasing, reformistic variety, combined with his unrealistically grandiose perspective and his love, mixed with fear, of democracy, blinded him.[8]

Tingsten knew nothing about economics and thought that democracy was opposed to socialization and a planned economy. It was from this perspective that he attacked the Social Democracy. But his lack of interest in pragmatic policy also constituted a moral strength. "Tingsten's greatness as a journalist was that he was there to preach the truth, not to achieve results."[9] In spite of the weaknesses that he criticized, Bo was full of admiration for Tingsten. His writings were always characterized by "a singular power, clarity and elegance. It is in this sense that his contributions remained at a constantly high level."[10] Bo's final verdict was superlative. "He is one of the few who cannot be imagined out of their time without it being changed."[11]

Den hierarkiska välfärden clearly demonstrated that Bo was a much better essayist than short story writer. While *Övertygelser* frequently feels artificial, the essay format allows him to develop the art of formulation which he abundantly possessed. The short stories offered few possibilities to display the irony, the erudition, the art of agitation, and the allusions which characterize *Den hierarkiska välfärden*. The latter book can still be read with pleasure, even given that with time Bo would completely change

---

[8] Södersten (1968b), p. 222.
[9] Ibid., p. 223.
[10] Ibid., pp. 224–25.
[11] Ibid., s 225.

his views with respect to which the forces were that created the wealth of the Swedish society. It was the first step into a genre that Bo would cultivate in the future: that of the debate essay.

Per Albin and the Brotherhood

In 1970, Bo again displayed his essay talents, by participating in a small book about Per Albin Hansson, the Swedish Prime Minister 1932–1936 and 1936–1946, *Per Albinlinjen* (*The Per Albin Way*).[12] Gunnar Fredriksson and Dieter Strand wanted to do an edited book on him and to that end contacted Kjell-Olof Feldt and Bo. Both accepted, but Feldt later changed his mind, so the end result was a book with three essays.[13] Bo's chapter is called "Per Albin och den socialistiska reformismen" ("Per Albin and Socialist Reformism"), one of Bo's most sympathetic and empathic essays, with a very rich content. Per Albin (as the Swedes knew him) has traditionally been considered a pragmatic tactician who kept the Socialist ideology in the background. Bo, however, argues that this view is erroneous.

Per Albin had his own political message. The central idea was that of the People's Home (folkhemmet), a home which should house all Swedes, an idea which has often been regarded as conservative. Bo argues that this interpretation is erroneous. It was much deeper than so, and it was based on Per Albin's dream of brotherhood. It was his most genuine and original political thought. The Socialist society had to rest on brotherhood, that is, equality, concern, cooperation, and help. It was no less than an attitude toward life which Per Albin wanted to turn into reality, and it was this attitude which was behind the idea of the People's Home. It made Per Albin turn away from both the elite and the bureaucracy. He wanted to enjoy the company of common people.

Bo relates how the new Swedish economic policy, based on the Keynesian message, took shape under Per Albin. He stresses that Per Albin understood that saving must increasingly take place under the aegis of the state. The Liberal and Conservative parties were convinced of the superiority of private enterprise and had not understood that society was an organism in perpetual development and that new organizational forms, with increasing state control, might be called for.

---

[12] Södersten (1970c).
[13] Interview with Gunnar Fredriksson, 12 February 2022.

Per Albin

Bo also deals with Per Albin's views of democracy: the thought that political democracy must have an economic counterpart and the highly original—somewhat strange—idea of a permanent government of national unity, where cooperation was the rule and where opposition would not take place only along party lines. The idea was difficult to explain but Bo contended that it was based on the view of society as an organism. The development of society was inexorable. As economic democracy was realized, the class struggle would gradually recede. Per Albin envisioned an ever more developed social policy and the control by society of the economy and of capital formation. The means of production would gradually be socialized, a development which would relegate the bourgeois parties to a position of perennial opposition. But here, brotherhood entered the picture: cooperation, consensus. Per Albin thought that it would be possible to do away with the old antagonism and create a new spirit of community, one where everybody accepted a Socialist order of society. The idea of a permanent government of national unity formed part of this vision.

Bo dodged the question of how realistic it was to believe that Liberals and Conservatives would accept the idea of a Socialist society without diehard opposition. Instead, he pointed to Per Albin as a model for the contemporary Social Democracy. The combination of a firm ideological conviction and an inquiring intellectual position was as necessary then as it was during the time when Per Albin headed the party.

REFORMIST SOCIALISM

In a newly written essay on reformist Socialism for his collection *Ut ur krisen* (*Out of the Crisis*) from 1981, Bo comes back to Per Albin and the brotherhood theme.[14] Reformism had made its breakthrough in the 1930s and Bo predicted that it would again be brought to the forefront in the 1980s. The extremely long period in power of the Social Democrats had led to an increased centralization of policy formulation within the party. Its commanding heights had obtained too much power. In 1976, however, its period in government was interrupted by the election triumph. This increased the polarization in Swedish politics. Conservative ideas were spread and at the same time, the trade unions were radicalized and demanded increased political influence.

Bo conceived of the situation as an opening for reformist Socialism. The issue was one of understanding the situation in order to be able to change it. The hegemony of the party was not given in any way, but it had to be defended and at times conquered anew. The reformist Socialism had to have a sharp ear for the prevailing ideological mood. Bo argued that the history of Socialism had always been characterized by a tension between centralism and decentralization. The former had grown stronger when politics had been professionalized and power had been concentrated to a small group. At the same time, however, Socialism needed decentralization. Reformist Socialism could not be built from the top. Bo came back to Per Albin Hansson's idea of brotherhood, "consideration, nearness, the will to understand and to encompass what is different, the individual."[15] The party had to see to it that the open discussion was kept alive within it and that it remained open to anybody, in order to break the bourgeois hegemony and substitute a Social Democratic one for it.

---

[14] "Reformistiskt 80tal" ("The Reformist 80s"), in Södersten (1981a).
[15] Ibid., p. 18.

CHAPTER 6

The Hunt for a Chair

Between 1968 and 1970, Bo applied for a number of professorships in Sweden and Denmark, without success, until the latter year, he got the August Röhss chair in Gothenburg. In 1968, two chairs were advertised at Stockholm University. Bo applied for both but was declared not qualified by all the three appointed experts, Ragnar Bentzel from Uppsala, Leif Johansen from Oslo, and Björn Thalberg from Lund. The following year, a chair in economics in Uppsala fell vacant after Tord Palander. The expert committee consisted of Harald Dickson from Gothenburg, Jørgen Gelting from Aarhus, Assar Lindbeck and Tord Palander, the retiring professor, a custom that was unfortunately common at the time. Again, Bo failed to meet the requirements as the committee saw it.

Lindbeck was mean.[1] He came back to Bo's dissertation. Neither the derivation of the results nor the presentation and the interpretation of them was satisfactory, and they could not be used for anything. Palander was even worse. He declared all the applicants not qualified. It was nothing short of a scandal that he was on the committee, after having made an absolute fool of himself in connection with the appointment of Ragnar Bentzel in 1965, where he completely contradicted his own previous judgments of the latter's qualifications in order to ensure that a student of

[1] Lindbeck (1969a).

his would get the position.[2] His judgment of Bo bordered on the defamatory.[3] He began by portraying Bo's production as dominated by an exceedingly simplified special case, the one with two countries, two commodities, and two factors, without mentioning that this was the dominant approach in the theory of international trade. He called the licentiate thesis primitive and impossible to apply to the Swedish economy, and the doctoral dissertation had received too high a grade. Bo did not understand what he was doing. Palander insinuated that the mathematical deductions were not his own. Bo had demonstrated a weakly developed ability to plan and carry out a theoretical scientific investigation. His mathematical and economic education was deficient and his production was one-sided.

The next position that Bo applied for was an associate professorship in Lund, where the expert committee consisted of three professors who had already passed judgment on him: Ragnar Bentzel, Björn Thalberg och Assar Lindbeck. This time he qualified, but he did not get the position. Bo appealed and called Lindbeck biased, after what had taken place in connection with his thesis defense in 1964, but to no avail.[4] During 1968, two chairs in economics had also fallen vacant at the University of Copenhagen, Bo applied for both. The committee which collectively—the Danish system differed from the Swedish one—evaluated the applicants consisted of professors Jørgen Gelting, Aarhus, Trygve Haavelmo, Oslo, Anders Ølgaard, Copenhagen and Poul Nørregaard Rasmussen, also Copenhagen, plus the chairman of the board of the Danish National Bank, Erik Hoffmeyer. Bo received a mixed evaluation. His thesis was seen as a valuable attempt of exact treatment of some central parts of the theory of international trade and to a certain extent also of some new problems, although the mathematical treatment was not successful. His textbook pointed to good knowledge about the new literature in the field, but it also had some defects. It was not enough, however. Bo did not get any of the Copenhagen chairs.[5]

. In 1969, the August Röhss chair in economics in Gothenburg was advertised, with a committee consisting of Guy Arvidsson from Lund Ragnar Bentzel and Anders Ølgaard. Bentzel still refused to declare Bo qualified, although he came pretty close, mainly because he did not think

---

[2] The story is told in the epilogue to Carlson and Lundahl (2019).
[3] Palander (1969).
[4] Södersten (1969c).
[5] Gelting et al. (1969).

that Bo dominated his analytical apparatus. The other two committee members, Arvidsson and Ølgaard, on the other hand, argued that Bo had been far too harshly judged by the former experts. Arvidsson contended that his dissertation had enough merits to warrant the grade of *docent*. He also praised the textbook manuscript, and in the end declared Bo qualified, with some hesitation.[6]

Anders Ølgaard was positive as well. In spite of its flaws, Bo's dissertation was a valuable contribution—the earlier evaluations had concentrated too much on formal defects—and he predicted that *International Economics* would get a wide international readership. Exactly like Arvidsson, considered Bo to qualify with some hesitation.[7] Both Arvidsson and Ølgaard ranked Bo ahead of his competitor, Karl Jungenfelt, which meant that he got the Gothenburg chair.

* * *

Fifty years afterward, the choice of expert committee members for the chairs that Bo applied for stands out as odd. Ragnar Bentzel served no less than there out of four times in connection with the Swedish positions, Assar Lindbeck and Björn Thalberg twice each, and Jørgen Gelting and Anders Ølgaard both once in Sweden and once in Denmark. It must certainly have been possible to find other experts within the Nordic countries so as to avoid completely predictable evaluations. This is the case not least with Bentzel and Lindbeck. It is difficult to get away from the suspicion that Bo's critical review of their book on housing may have influenced their view of him. Drafting them in such a situation, not only once but several times, points to a good deal of bad judgment among the faculties which appointed them, an impression which is confirmed by Guy Arvidsson's and Anders Ølgaard's conclusion in connection with the Gothenburg chair, that Bo had been far too harshly treated by the previous committees.

---

[6] Arvidsson (1970).
[7] Ølgaard (1970).

The Swedish Institute for Social Research

From 1 January 1971, Bo Södersten was professor of economics in Gothenburg. He immediately took leave of absence, however. The reason was that the Institute for Labour Market Research at Stockholm University would be reorganized. Bo was appointed expert and secretary of the committee which worked on the issue. The Swedish Institute for Social Research (Institutet för social forskning [SOFI]) began its activities on 1 January 1972 with Bo Södersten as acting director until a professor of labor market policy could be appointed. Labor market policy was not Bo's field, but during his time at SOFI and shortly thereafter, he wrote a couple of essays on this theme.[8]

The first one, "Socialpolitik och ekonomisk politik" ("Social Policy and Economic Policy"), discusses the delimitation and function of social policy and its relation to the general economic policy. Bo focuses on the intervention with the market income formation in order to change the distribution of incomes and consumption and he discusses the impotence of traditional social policy measures during periods of mass unemployment. He defines the core of social policy as "problems of social insurance and loss of income, revalidation, social allowance, welfare, mechanisms of social exclusion, etc."[9] The issue is to build methods to tackle these problems against the background of a more general economic and sociological context. Bo then surveys the development of employment in the 1960s and early 1970s and the new "natural unemployment" approach to employment which claims that full employment in principle is impossible. Which were the consequences of this for social policy? Would it have to be concentrated on the problems caused by the existence of a lower class?

The second article, "Modern inflations-och arbetslöshetsteori" ("Modern Inflation and Unemployment Theory"), contrasted the Keynesian recipe for full employment with the natural unemployment approach and the role of expectations in the latter. Economic policy measures to reduce unemployment would simply result in the adaptation of the expectations of the economic actors and the economy would revert to the natural rate of unemployment. At the same time, a new microeconomic theory of search unemployment had seen the daylight, according to

---

[8] Reprinted in Södersten (1975).
[9] Ibid., p. 133.

which unemployment during a period of search for a new job was not unproductive.

When the focus of the new institute for social research had been defined, a chair in social policy was advertised. Since Bo had been acting director of the institute, it was obvious that he would apply, in the hope that his work on the creation of it and his subsequent year there would guarantee that he would get the position. Things, however, did not turn out that way. Seven serious candidates applied and were scrutinized by an expert committee consisting of Erik Lundberg, Lars Werin, and Bent Rold Andersen. Lundberg declared Bo not qualified, arguing that his production was highly uneven, ranging from "excellent efforts to directly demeritorious works." He was weak when it came to empirical and institutional analysis and had not published anything in the field of social policy.[10] Lars Werin also pointed out that Bo had few publications in social policy. His overall competence in economics might qualify him, but this was not enough.[11] Bent Rold Andersen, finally, found Bo qualified, but only with considerable doubt. Again, the problem was Bo's lack of publications in the relevant field. Andersen declared him qualified on the basis of his general merits but did not put him among the leading candidates.[12] The chair instead went to Gösta Rehn, a person with a solid background in labor market and social policy issues.[13]

During the next few years, Bo published a couple of articles related to social policy. The first, from 1975, was written together with Nancy Barrett. It compared unemployment patterns in the United States and Sweden, "Unemployment Flows, Welfare and Labor Market Efficiency in Sweden and the United States,"[14] where unemployment is split into two components: the average number of times that a person has been unemployed in a year and the average duration of the unemployment. The welfare implications differed between the two components. In the former case, it was possible that the unemployed person wanted to get a new job while in the second case there was a risk that he or she had problems finding a job.

---

[10] Lundberg (1972), p. 26.
[11] Werin (1972).
[12] Andersen (1972).
[13] For a biography of Rehn, see Erixon and Wadensjö (2013).
[14] Barrett and Södersten (1975).

The unemployment pattern differed between the two countries. Americans were unemployed more often, but Swedes were unemployed for longer periods. In the United States, new jobs were found faster than in Sweden. Nancy and Bo did, however, not conclude that things were better in the United States. The statistics did not allow for a clear-cut division into voluntary and unvoluntary unemployment.

Three years later, Bo published an article about the situation of the Swedish women in the labor market.[15] Their labor market participation had increased from 32 percent in 1960 to 50 percent in 1975, an increase which Bo called unique in history. In order to explain this development, he resorted to the "new household economics" developed above all by Gary Becker which claims that the decisions about participation in the labor market are made by the household, and not by the individuals. When real incomes and education increase, so does the income loss that you make by not working, which tends to increase the extent of female participation in the labor market. Bo was, however, skeptical to Becker's approach. Attitudes toward work had changed as well: security, equality, and independence, as well as demonstration effects: other women worked.

Gothenburg and Lund

After failing to get the chair in social policy in Stockholm, Bo had to return to Gothenburg. He taught there in 1973–1974, commuting to Lund, where he continued to have his family. In 1974–1975, he again was on leave, serving as visiting professor at the American University in Washington, DC, and as a visiting researcher at Harvard. When he returned to Sweden, he finally moved to Gothenburg, in the fall of 1975.

Bo came back to a deeply divided department. It had gathered a large number of Marxist teachers and students. Most of the Marxists on the faculty had been placed in the "C" corridor, commonly known as the Ho Chi Minh Trail. Since Bo had never liked Marxists and made no secret of his feelings, it was inevitable that sooner or later it would come to serious clashes. Many Marxists had moved to Roskilde in Denmark, to the new radical University Centre, founded in 1972, which acted as a magnet on academics with a leftist inclination. This meant that not all those left in Gothenburg were first rate. Some had been assistants for a decade or more,

---

[15] Södersten (1978b). The same paper was presented in English at a meeting of the International Economic Association and was published as Södersten (1980c).

and Bo was determined to clean out the nest by forcing them either to take courses or present dissertation drafts. This, of course, provoked lots of resistance. At the time, a series of experiments with democratization of the university departments was going on in Sweden, and Gothenburg had one of the more extreme forms, with heavy representation of students and administrative personnel and frequent elections to the department board. Every time, a number of Marxist sympathizers registered for studies at the economics department, and then the mudslinging began.

Bo had had a premonition of what his years in Gothenburg would possibly be like. In the presentation of economics which he wrote for his installation as a professor, he finished by exhorting the Marxists to concentrate on publication of scientific results and stop being provincial.[16] The worst moments were when positions were up for grabs in the department. This inevitably led to confrontation and letters to the university administration.[17] In an interview in *Göteborgs-Posten* in 1977, Bo stated his views on Marxism, at a time when the department was again involved in a bitter struggle about a lectureship. Marxism was nothing but a religious salvation doctrine. It was a political ideology, and Marxist research was conspicuous by its absence.[18] Bo lost his last battle in the Gothenburg, which ended with a letter to the government signed by eighteen researchers and teachers who accused him of attempting to stop the careers of good academics on political grounds.[19]

In 1978, Bo left Gothenburg without regret. In 1976, Torsten Gårdlund, who had been professor of international economics in Lund since 1965, retired and his position was advertised. Bo applied. The expert committee consisted of Gårdlund himself and the two Norwegians Jan Serck-Hanssen and Tore Thonstad. This time, nobody could threaten Bo. The three experts briefly recapitulated the evaluation made in 1970 of his qualification in economics for the Gothenburg chair, when there were doubts with respect to his merits. In 1976, the situation was different. In the first place, the chair was in his special branch of economics: international economics. Bo had worked mainly with international trade but also, to some extent, with development economics, another of the core areas

---

[16] Södersten (1973b), p. 33.
[17] For a thoughtful account, from the Marxist camp, of Bo's time in the Gothenburg department, see Lönnroth (2011).
[18] Franck (1977).
[19] Ibid.

included in the definition of the chair. Secondly, he had increased his scientific output. The overall picture of him was mixed, but overwhelmingly positive. The joint summary evaluation of his qualifications stated:

> Summing up, it must be said that Södersten had demonstrated an ability to choose clearly delimited research tasks and derive results from his works. He possesses considerable knowledge within the area of the professorship, has made valuable pedagogical contributions and has participate actively in the debate on economic policy. His main weakness is that it may seem that he does not always dominate completely the mathematical models that he uses, and mistakes occur both in his scientific works and his textbooks. In most cases, however, these mistakes are not very serious.[20]

The expert committee unanimously declared Bo qualified for the chair and put him first. He was appointed professor of international economics from 1 July 1977.

---

[20] Notat (1977), p. 6.

CHAPTER 7

The Housing Market

Bo's third scientific monograph deals with the housing market in Sweden. The book—*Betalt för att bo* (*Paid for Dwelling*)—published in 1978 is co-authored with Bo Sandelin,[1] who the year before had defended his doctoral dissertation, *Prisutveckling och kapitalvinster på bostadsfastigheter* (*Price Developments and Capital Gains in the Housing Market*), at the University of Gothenburg .[2] Bo Södersten had not dropped the housing theme after his review of the book by Bentzel, Lindbeck, and Ståhl but had written a number of articles in daily newspapers which dealt with the income and wealth redistribution caused with the price increases in the housing market.

In *Betalt för att bo*, Bo and Bo provide times series from the 1950s to the 1970s which demonstrate that the average homeowner had made a good profit on his house, after all costs had been deducted. This they compared with the costs that the tenants in the housing market had incurred during the same period. The prices of single-family houses had increased with 13 percent 1973–1976, faster than the general price level, while the prices of tenant houses had increased slower than the latter.

---

[1] Sandelin and Södersten (1978).
[2] Sandelin (1977).

Paid for dwelling

Which were the causes of this development? The population had grown, and home construction had been concentrated on multi-family houses, while that of one-family houses had been lagging. Building costs had increased rapidly, which in turn had affected the level of rents. This had made people turn to the market for one-family houses. The increased building costs were the result of a relatively slow development of productivity in the construction sector. The price increases on small houses had a wealth effect. Bo and Bo present series both for implicit (unrealized) gains and realized profits.

Real Estate Taxation

The presentation of the situation in the market for small houses ends with a discussion of the taxation of the gains on one-family houses. The latter were either not taxed at all or taxed at a lower rate than other incomes. Such gains, however, Bo and Bo suggested, should be taxed either in the same way as other incomes, or harder, since they were work-free incomes. The dwelling costs differed between multi-family and one-family houses. The homeowner, but not the tenant, made a profit from living in his house. He built up a claim, a claim which he could realize at any time. As soon as he sold his house this claim turned into a realized profit. "The gilded road to wealth in recent years in our country is not work. Wealth is obtained by obtaining a large work-free income via homeownership."[3]

A reform was needed. The amount of houses built and their distribution between multi-family and one-family houses was to a large extent determined by the tax system and the latter favored one-family houses. Bo and Bo suggested that the taxation of housing should be founded on the principle that the dwellers should pay the cost per unit of time for the services rendered by their dwellings. For reasons of equality—so as not to lock out groups with small economic resources from one-family houses, all purchases of houses should be completely (100 percent) financed by loans. Anyone who could pay the current costs of a small house should be allowed to finance his purchase through the credit market.

The taxation of housing should be nominal. The tying of the purchase value to the cost of living which existed at the time should be abolished so that profits on housing were taxed like other incomes. These profits did not spring from factors which the individual homeowners could influence and should hence be taxed when realized. Bo and Bo advocated a 40 percent tax on realized profits. In addition, the current services rendered by the dwellings had to be taxed. The standard revenue at the time was 3 percent of the assessed value, which corresponded to about 2 percent of the market value. In order to achieve parity with the bank rate of interest (the alternative investment), the standard ought to be raised to 7 percent of the assessed value. Altogether, Bo and Bo argued, their suggested changes would lead to a drastic reduction of the inequalities in the housing market.

It was inevitable that the Sandelin-Södersten book would arouse the sentiments of the homeowners. It ended up on top of the placard of the largest daily newspaper in Sweden, and it received a lot of attention also in regional and local newspapers. The book was also criticized in the Social Democratic ideological journal, *Tiden*, for confusing realized and unrealized profits, for not taking the importance of location into account and for taxing low-income earners out of the market for one-family houses.

---

[3] Sandelin and Södersten (1978), p. 106.

Besides, the book did not deal with the condominium market at all—a market where the same kind of profits were made as in the small house market.[4]

After the Book

Bo continued to write about the housing market after the publication of *Betalt för att bo*. He then extended his perspective to the determination of rental levels in the regulated housing market.[5] These aimed at balancing the housing standards and rentals and did not take into account the attraction of the location. The preferences of the housing consumers were not allowed to come into play. The rent control created an excess demand. The dwelling was considered a social right, which from the point of view of location led to grave injustices. Contacts, nepotism, and favoritism determined the distribution of the available apartments. To argue that a free determination of the rental level would lead to segregation made no sense. It was impossible to achieve equality in each individual market in the economy. People's preferences for housing and consumption of other goods differed, and there was no unequivocally "fair" way of distributing apartments.

A book chapter from 1990, written together with Arne Karyd, demonstrates that on the macroeconomic level, the goal of the Swedish housing policy had been reached in the mid-1970s. Sweden had more and larger dwellings per thousand inhabitants than other comparable countries, which had led to a drastic reduction of construction. The extent of subsidization of housing had increased markedly since then. Tax and interest subsidies distorted the housing market and led to unwanted redistribution of incomes and wealth.

The tax subsidies were indirect. The house owners could deduct interest payments in their income declarations, which lowered the government revenue. Their magnitude could not be calculated, to some extent they financed other expenditures than those on housing, and they redistributed incomes in favor of the homeowners. The interest subsidies, in turn, went directly from the state to the real estate owners. Their purpose was to keep the cost of newly produced apartments down, but Arne and Bo argued

---

[4] Lindgren (1978).
[5] Södersten (1989c).

that it would be preferable to let higher rents for more attractive apartments finance the construction of new houses.

Besides, building with the aid of interest subsidies was not the most efficient way of establishing an equilibrium in the housing market. Market rents would lead to higher real estate prices in attractive areas, prices which would cover the costs of construction. Interest rate subsidies could be defended only for less attractive locations. It was impossible not to take location into account. Regulation of the market would simply lead to the absurd situation that two apartments which differed with respect to the attraction of the neighborhood would have the same price. Black or semi-black markets for apartment exchange would arise, and the results of administratively determined access to apartments were not in any way better than those of the free market. The old argument that the housing shortage could be "built away" was completely crazy. Of course, a deregulated housing market would have consequences for the distribution of incomes, but it would lead to the production of houses preferred by the consumers, and it would free resources for other useful projects in society.[6]

[6] Karyd and Södersten (1990).

CHAPTER 8

The Dream of the Labor-Managed Economy

An issue which exerted a great deal of attraction on Bo Södersten during the 1970s was one of the labor-managed economy. In 1970, Jaroslav Vanek at Cornell University had published a book on the theory of the labor-managed firm.[1] Bo had read it and become sold on the idea of a decentralized Socialism. During the 1970s, he wrote a number of articles where he presented the main features of the theory and discussed its applicability on the Swedish economy.

The first ones were short newspaper chronicles in *Aftonbladet*.[2] Bo discerned two main roads along which the advancement toward the labor-managed economy ought to proceed. One was that of increased influence of the employees in their companies. The second went via control of the capital formation, for example, by purchase of shares through collective funds. He thought that the Social Democrats had been too cautious and hesitant. "The time has come to demonstrate that a consequent application of Social Democratic ideology implies a deep-going change of society. Capitalism has done its duty. Capitalism can go."[3]

[1] Vanek (1970).
[2] Reprinted in *Den svenska sköldpaddan* (Södersten 1975).
[3] Ibid., p. 193.

The articles in *Aftonbladet* were followed by a few longer persuasive ones. The first one points to labor-managed firms as an alternative both to the centralized Communist economy and to traditional capitalism.[4] The guiding principle of the labor-managed firm was that it should maximize the net income per worker (the gross income minus the cost of capital) instead of profits. This is, however, not problem-free, but will provoke a "perverse" reaction to product price increases. This backward-bending supply curve builds on two conflicting tendencies. On the one hand, you want as many workers as possible in the company in order to minimize the capital cost per worker. On the other hand, you want as few workers as possible, since this increases the production value per worker. An increase of the product price reinforces the latter tendency at the expense of the former. Hence, those already working in the company attempt to reduce their numbers or at least not let any newcomers in. Production may decrease and investment may suffer. To solve this problem, new companies must be created, but this will not occur spontaneously in labor-managed economies, but a certain degree of central direction may be necessary. Bo, however, doubted that the tendency to shed labor was very strong in practice. He confided in worker solidarity.

The Problem of Capital Formation

In the labor-managed economy, capital would be collectively owned. The workers of the individual company would decide how the investments within the latter were made, but they should not own the company directly but pay interest on the capital that it had borrowed from the "social fund" that owned it. The collective ownership would make incomes much more equal than in the capitalist economy. The incentive structure would also be different. Whereas the worker in the capitalist company would minimize his effort given his wage since the result of an increased effort will accrue to the capitalist owners, in the labor-managed firm they would maximize their effort since the increases will result in higher labor incomes. This follows from the maximization principle of the labor-managed firm. Bo romanticized work within this firm. The workers would work together for the common good, assume collective responsibility for the company they all owned, and support each other.

[4] Södersten (1973a).

The reasoning is, however, not convincing. As Mancur Olson had demonstrated several years before, in a classic book, the result will probably rather be the opposite one.[5] Since everybody gets a share in the result of the increased effort of the individual worker, everybody will wait for everybody else to do something. The net income of the company is a collective good for the employees, which nobody can be excluded from. Hence, the production of the company tends to be lower than the optimum, and the larger the company, the more serious will probably this problem be.[6]

When Bo Södersten published his book of essays *Den svenska sköldpaddan* (*The Swedish Turtle*) in 1975, he included a newly written essay "Industripolitik för arbetarstyre" ("Industrial Policy for Labor Management"), where he linked the need for industrial finance with the need that he perceived of a transition from a capitalist economic system to a system which rested on public control but without undue centralization.[7] This essay is arguably the most ideological one that he ever wrote. In it he paints the future society that he wanted to see, in a way which had a lot in common with the visions of the utopian Socialists of the ideal society, a society where the humans controlled their existence, were satisfied with what they did, and felt well in general.

Bo's point of departure was that the Swedish Social Democrats had neglected the need for a coherent industrial policy which controlled industrial investment. The measure that Bo suggested was labor-managed firms combining worker influence and equality with efficiency. The group most interested in and most dependent on the success of the companies was neither the capitalists nor the state. It was the workers. For this reason, you could expect labor-managed firms to work well. The overwhelming part of the investment in the industrial sector was financed by profits, and it was not in any way possible to contend that it was simply the management and the capital owners who created the profits. Therefore, the influence of the employees had to increase, via increased representation on the company boards—a majority representation.

The criteria that should govern the activities of the labor-managed companies should, on the one hand, be payment of the agreed wages and, on the other hand, an investment pace that was satisfactory both from the business point of view and from the point of view of society. The existing

---

[5] Olson (1965).
[6] For criticisms of Bo's article, see Horvat (1974) and Eidem and Viotti (1974).
[7] Södersten (1975).

capital stock must be maintained and new investment must be made to ensure expansion and modernization. The labor-managed firms must cooperate with the state and take socioeconomic criteria into account when making investment decisions. Economic progress rests on structural change because society is subject to change all the time. This would come easier in the labor-managed economy, since the solidarity principle governing the activities of the individual firms could be extended to solidarity also *between* firms. An efficient industrial sector was in the interest of all employees. However, the establishment of new companies was not a spontaneous process but required an active policy. It implied risk-taking, it had to be coordinated by a central organization and had to be financed by a credit institute which could mobilize the necessary funds.

Throughout his essay, Bo had presented economic arguments for the superiority of the labor-managed economy in relation to the capitalist alternative, whose historical role, he contended, had come to an end. However, the strongest arguments for a transition to labor management were found on a different level, harder to grasp:

> There are large groups in our society, mainly blue- and white-collar workers within the large wage-earning collectives who at present do not get a reasonable chance to realize their creative power and their energy. The labor-managed economy could free large quantities of energy, creative power and organizational talent.
>
> With labor management, many firms would undergo a considerable vitalization. [...] The social control would work positively, as a spur and as encouragement. All the workers would feel that they themselves, and no outsiders, who controlled the company.[8]

Bo's final words breathe both humanism and Socialism:

> A transition to labor management does not solve all problems. But it should solve several and above all do away with the fundamental opposition that exists between the economic organization of capitalism and all aspirations towards equality, brotherhood and humanity.
>
> A labor-managed economy will restore the value and dignity of work. It constitutes the form of economic organization which may constitute the foundation of the fully developed Socialist society.[9]

---

[8] Ibid., p. 56.
[9] Ibid., p. 57.

Micro Aspects

Bo Södersten returned to the labor-managed economy in another long article, in 1976, which dealt with micro aspects.[10] He made three comparisons between labor-managed and traditionally organized firms. The first dealt with the increased participation and influence over the own work situation. Bo compared the Scientific Management school that aimed at standardized work routines, a simple organization of the work that made it easy to measure and monitor, and the sociological and sociopsychological Human Relations literature which strongly indicated that influence over the own work situation had a positive influence on both production and well-being and which hence spoke in favor of labor management. It made work meaningful and increased the solidarity with the company. These gains had to be compared with the cost increases caused by the new form of organization, due, for example, to the fact that the employees had to spend more time on the management of the firm. When the productivity-increasing and cost-increasing effects balanced each other at the margin, the optimal form of organization had been reached.

Bo also discussed the role of education in the labor-managed firms. In capitalist companies, the on-the-job training tended to be under-dimensioned since it was impossible to prevent the employees from moving. All the returns on this training did not accrue to the company. In the labor-managed firm, the propensity to move would be lower, since the extent of solidarity of the workers with the company would be higher. Both the capitalist and the labor-managed firm aimed at technical progress, but the character of the latter differed between the two systems. The capitalist companies aimed for improvements which made it easier to monitor work and increase profits, while the latter would opt for changes that increased productivity by a better organization of the steering process characterized by worker influence. This would increase both the efficiency of the control of the workers of the company and their satisfaction with the work. Possibly, but the argument does not feel quite convincing.

Finally, Bo raised the issue of why we had not yet arrived at labor management if the latter was a superior form of organization. A possible answer was that there was no open competition between different organization principles. The institutions in society had been designed in order to cooperate with the already existing organization forms. Thus, it was not

---

[10] Södersten (1976b).

certain that labor-managed firms would be able to obtain credit. Especially at the beginning of their existence they would have problems raising the necessary securities. It was also probable that the existing educational system would not produce the type of education needed by these firms. The introduction of labor management would hence hardly be possible unless the society underwent fundamental changes.

WAGE-EARNERS' FUNDS

The issue of labor management was intimately related to the need for industrial investment, since the latter was what determined Sweden's ability to compete in international markets, the rate of growth and thus, in the end, employment.[11] The investment decisions had been left to the capitalists, but decisions made in this way did not correspond to the future needs of society. New methods were required, notably employee influence. It did not make sense to concentrate the ambitions of the labor movement just on wage bargaining. This, in 1975, had led to a 40 percent wage increase over two years, an outcome which was catastrophic from the point of view of economic stability but for the workers to assume their responsibility toward society and reduce their demands they had to be offered something else instead: influence over the investment policy of the companies. Here, the much-debated wage-earners' funds came into the picture. They could contribute to the resolution of the conflict between growth and equity inherent to the capitalist system and also to the foundation of a rational investment policy aiming toward the longer run.

The wage-earners' funds were based on arguments of equality and justice. Bo shared this view.[12] A tiny minority of people controlled the Swedish economy. A redistribution of incomes was necessary. It was of course not possible to rule out income differences in the labor-managed economy. Profitability would differ between companies, but in the labor-managed economy, incomes would be directly related to the labor effort. The large existing income differences were due to the relative wealth of the individuals, but in the labor-managed economy, with time, all income would be labor income.

---

[11] Södersten (1976c).
[12] Södersten (1976d).

In 1977, Bo presented a practical proposal of how the wage earners could get more influence over investments.[13] His idea was that some kind of investment committees should be created. He presented it in more detail during a political speech on the first of May the same year. The committees should consist of both owner employee representatives, with the latter in the majority: five versus four from the owner side. The money would come from the future wage increases—one-third—to be managed by the committees over periods of five years at the time.[14]

Two years later, in 1979, in one of his last essays on the subject, Bo asked whether Sweden was on its way toward the labor-managed economy.[15] He linked the issue to the debate about the wage-earners' funds that was raging at the time. Those whose attitude toward the latter was positive should also embrace the idea of labor management. He found it strange that in a situation where the security of employment had increased and employee representatives had been introduced on the company boards, labor management had attracted so little interest and he came back to the importance of cooperation between labor-managed enterprises and the state. He rejected the proposals of a tripartite—owners, state, employees—collaboration which had been presented around the same time. That would simply lead to a collision between the principles of profit maximization and maximization of the net income per employee and possibly some vaguely defined public interest. Firms had to be governed by a single principle.

The capitalists had to be phased out, and Bo did not accept direct state representation. The introduction of bureaucratic controls would simply reduce the efficiency of the firms. In the end, it was difficult to conceive of the wage-earners' funds without labor management. The latter could be applied to a number of public enterprises as well—those operating directly in markets or under market-like conditions. The state could purchase goods and services from labor-managed firms, a principle that would reduce the risk of bureaucratic mismanagement. The political function—goal formulation and control—could then be separated from the executive one. Bo was not particularly optimistic when it came to the possibility of introducing labor-managed firms in Sweden. The fundamental principles were not well enough known, and the international experience, for

---

[13] Södersten (1977a, 1977b).
[14] Bege (1977).
[15] Södersten (1979b), English version in Södersten (1982b).

example, from Mondragón in the Basque Country and Yugoslavia, had not received enough publicity. In the Swedish debate, labor management had been depicted as a threat to the pluralistic society. Bo considered this nothing but scare tactics. It was difficult to conceive of a more decentralized decision method than the one represented by the labor-managed enterprises. They had, however, ended up in the shadow of the idea of tripartite representation, an idea which threatened to bureaucratize the economy. Bo was not certain that Sweden was ready for a transition to labor management in the 1980s. The risk was high that the politicians would instead dump the responsibility for the economy on bureaucrats, company managers, and public authorities.

The labor-managed economy was Bo Södersten's principal contribution to the political debate in Sweden. Regardless of your political stance, it must be admitted that he had taken great care to build his argument, an argument which rested both on economic analysis and on his—somewhat romantic—perception of the political realities of the 1970s—a perception which he had to modify over the years when he realized that the public opinion in Sweden might not share his views.

A Utopian Idea

The idea of labor management stood out as utopian in several ways. In a critique of Bo's first major article on the subject, Rolf Eidem and Staffan Viotti questioned whether labor-managed enterprises really were superior to the traditional capitalistic ones.[16] If so, they should not only have been established but should also have out-competed the latter. It was not at all certain that there would be any fundamental organizational differences between the two systems. Wouldn't labor-managed enterprises also be forced to resort to more or less hierarchic forms of organization, exactly like the capitalist firms? And what evidence was there that no shirking would take place in the labor-managed companies? Shirking is hard to detect and measure when the company operations rest on team production. That the distribution of income would become more equal in a labor-managed economy was a distinct possibility, but Bo did not provide any analysis of the welfare effects of the transition.

Eidem and Viotti were also skeptical of the process whereby new firms would be established. It was hardly credible that existing companies would

[16] Eidem and Viotti (1974).

help competitors to enter the market, and the centralization of the creation of firms was something that Bo wanted to avoid. Nor did they believe that labor-managed firms would be more eager than capitalist ones to share their research and development results with others.

The dream of the labor-managed economy was a beautiful dream of a Socialist society with a more human face than the centralized command economy which rested exclusively on coercion or the capitalist economy with its inherent inequalities of income and wealth. But it was no more than a dream—a piece of wishful thinking, if you like. It is clear that Bo assumed the existence of a number of mechanisms and attitudes that are not likely to exist in real life. Gradually he realized this, and gradually he chose to drop the idea. As we will see below, later in his life he would be converted into a staunch supporter of the capitalist economy.

CHAPTER 9

Contrasting Economies: Sweden and the Developing Countries

More Textbooks

Spurred by good royalty incomes from his book on international economics, Bo embarked on more textbook projects. The first one was an anthology about the Swedish economy, *Svensk ekonomi* (*The Swedish Economy*). The purpose was to provide a picture of its structure and development. The perspective was wide: one hundred years of Swedish development, the credit market, growth and structural change during the postwar period, stabilization policy, resource allocation in the public sector, industrial policy and the regional structural problems, environmental policy, and, finally, Sweden in the international economy and our position vis-à-vis the developing countries. *Svensk ekonomi* was published in three editions between 1970 and 1982.[1] In the later editions, chapters were added on monetary policy and the place of women in the Swedish economy. The book was used in several Swedish universities.

In the fall of 1981, when giving a first-year course in macroeconomics, Bo realized that American textbooks were unsatisfactory from the Swedish point of view. Almost without exception, they dealt with a closed economy, without foreign trade, a reasonable simplification as far as the

---

[1] Södersten (1970b, 1974a, 1982a).

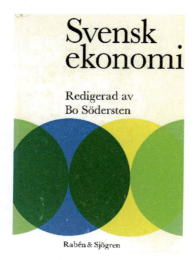

The Swedish economy

American economy was concerned, but not for Sweden, with its large foreign trade in relation to GDP, and, of course, American textbooks had nothing to say about Swedish economic policy—a clear disadvantage for Swedish students, whose first priority should be to learn how to analyze the problems of their own country.

Bo drew the conclusion that a Swedish textbook was needed and immediately set about writing it with the aid of Lennart Berg, Sten Magnusson, and Bo Sandelin. In 1983, *Makroekonomi och stabiliseringspolitik* (*Macroeconomics and Stabilization Policy*) was finished.[2] The point of departure for the book was stabilization policy, notably the ambitious Swedish employment policy and the fight against inflation. The book is mainly traditional Keynesian with IS-LM analysis, the accelerator-multiplicator model, and the effects of fiscal and monetary policy. The open economy and the problem of equilibrating the balance of payments are discussed as well as the foreign currency market and theories of devaluation.

---

[2] Södersten (1983). When the time came to print the book, Bo and his assistant, Tarmo Haavisto, went to the printer's office to discuss the layout. Tarmo reported the outcome: "No letters were too large for Södersten's name and none too small for Sandelin's."

Macroeconomics and stabilization policy

The longest chapter of the book deals with labor market and inflation problems, the Phillips curve and stagflation, as well as the specific Swedish analysis of wage formation and inflation in disaggregated terms—one sector subject to competition and one protected sector—rational expectations and fixed versus flexible exchange rates. Another central chapter is devoted to the relation between means and ends in economic policy, internal and external balance in the Swedish context.

Makroekonomi och stabiliseringspolitik mainly builds on the Keynesian approach to macroeconomics, but a couple of alternative approaches are also dealt with. One is monetarism, with its emphasis of the influence of the money supply on economic fluctuations and its questioning of the Phillips curve. The second one stands out as somewhat odd in the context: growth accounting. Bo's book deals mainly with short-run stabilization problems, but growth accounting is concerned with the separation of the long-term effects on economic growth of population growth, capital accumulation, and disembodied technical progress.

In 1987, five years had passed since the last edition of *Svensk ekonomi* had been published. That year, Bo replaced this anthology by a new one: *Marknad och politik* (*Markets and Politics*). The new anthology saw six editions, the last one in 2004, before Bo passed the editorship on to Hans

The Swedish economy again

Tson Söderström.[3] The purpose of the book was to highlight the changes that had taken place in the Swedish market in recent years, to show how the most important markets worked, to highlight the functioning of the public sector and the tax system and how these interacted with the private sector of the economy. To this was added growth and stabilization problems and, in later editions, environmental policy, the health sector, the place of Sweden in the international economy, trade and direct investment, the welfare state and entrepreneurship. Bo himself wrote about the Swedish policy toward developing countries in the first three editions, and thereafter about Sweden, the EU, and the EMU. With time, a book was created which covered most aspects of the Swedish economy and its problems. The concept was sustainable. The book kept its place on the course reading lists. The latest edition so far, the twelfth one, was published in 2017, edited by Lars Hultkrantz and Pär Österholm.[4]

---

[3] Södersten (1987a, 1990a, 1996a, 1997a, 2000a), Södersten and Söderström (2004).
[4] Hultkrantz and Österholm (2017).

Economic Development

Bo Södersten's specialty was international economics. The step from there to development economics was a small one, given that the insertion of the latter into the international economy had a strong domestic impact. In Lund, the chair in international economics was defined in such a way as to explicitly incorporate development as well. Bo, however, never produced any major work in development economics, only a number of articles and book chapters, and on two occasions, he worked as a consultant to SIDA on development issues.

Already in his licentiate thesis, Bo demonstrated that he was interested in long-term economic development, both theoretically and empirically. He returned to the development theme several times during his career. Not least did he write about Swedish economic development. Bo stressed that we had had uninterrupted and steady growth for a hundred years, between 1870 and 1970, but that the Swedish growth machine had thereafter begin to stall. He also dealt with the problems of the developing countries, an interest manifested mainly in reports from journeys to such countries and in a couple of consultancy reports.

In 1974, Bo and I edited a two-volume anthology on economic development, *Utvecklingsekonomi (Development Economics)*, *Underutvecklingens mekanismer (The Mechanisms of Underdevelopment)*, and *Planering och resursmobilisering (Planning and Resource Mobilization)*,[5] with a second, revised, one-volume, edition in 1979.[6] They constituted the first attempt by Swedish economists to present a coherent view of the development problem, and they remained on the university course lists for a few years.

How should the development problem be tackled? The year before Bo and I published our anthology, a government committee presented a report which proposed to earmark some of the Swedish aid money for research on developing countries.[7] We read it and found that it left a few things to be desired, above all when it came to the identification and presentation of the main development problems. Hence, we wrote a critical article in *Ekonomisk Debatt*.[8] We thought that the report dealt far too much with underdevelopment as a multidimensional problem and that it had missed that the development issue in the end was a matter of mass

[5] Lundahl and Södersten (1974b, 1974c),
[6] Lundahl and Södersten (1979).
[7] SOU 1973:41.
[8] Lundahl and Södersten (1974a).

poverty, the mechanisms behind this poverty, and finding ways to reduce it and increase the standard of living of broad population segments. The development problem was mainly economic, which the report had missed, presumably because no economist had been involved in its writing.

Development economics

Bo was impressed by the neo-institutional approach to economic history represented by people like Douglass North and Nathan Rosenberg which he came back to in several newspaper articles.[9] At the beginning of the sixteenth century, the West was not economically ahead of other civilizations like China and Islam, but thereafter the paths began to diverge. The West managed to build institutions that facilitated growth-inducing international trade and exchange. Most important of all was that the rulers could be tamed so that they could no longer deprive the productive forces of the fruits of their labor. It took the West 300 years to build good institutions. Other nations failed to adopt these institutions and hence remained poor.

In two publications from 1993 and 1994, Bo surveys the relation between education, institutions, and growth.[10] Modern economic growth had its roots in good institutions, one of which was education. It began to be developed at the beginning of the sixteenth century. Bo uses the "old"

---

[9] The approach is presented in Södersten (1991g) and Södersten (1999a).
[10] Södersten (1993a, 1994a).

growth theory, where technical progress is exogenous, all countries can accumulate capital and incomes tend to converge over time, as his point of departure. The empirical material, however, rather indicated that the income gap would widen.

To explain this, a "new" type of growth theory was needed, one where the growth-generating factors were endogenous.[11] Knowledge is produced, and it is used by firms. The knowledge of an individual depends not only on his own education but also on that of his colleagues, and it can be used by many people simultaneously. This tends to have strong growth effects, especially if it results in new production functions with increasing returns to scale. Bo tied the effects of education to the Swedish industrialization process: a process driven, on the one hand, by capital accumulation and, on the other, by a modernization of the universities in the direction of natural sciences. Improved education in turn interacted with good institutions which facilitated international trade.

Income distribution was a theme that had engaged Bo for a long time, not least in his dissertation and in some of his ideological shorter articles. In 1974, he brought up the relation between economic development and income distribution in an article in *Tiden*.[12] The inequalities within poor countries were often wider than those within rich countries, inequalities that had a heavy impact on the living conditions of poor people. Bo was not particularly optimistic with respect to the future. Positive effects of capital accumulation could easily be swamped by labor-saving technical progress. Even such an innovation as the Green Revolution seemed to have dubious distribution effects. Only large farmers could afford the irrigation and mechanization that was often required to make the miracle seed profitable. It was difficult to get a more equal distribution of incomes without changing the entire political and economic system in poor countries, and not even then it was certain that the living standard would increase.

In 1990, Bo Södersten participated in a symposium which compared the development of the Nordic and Latin American countries over a century.[13] He then dealt with the Swedish *siglo de oro*, the period 1870–1970, a century when Swedish growth was only surpassed by that of Japan. His essay tells the story of the industrialization of Sweden up to the First World

---

[11] Bo makes reference to Romer (1986, 1990a, 1990b) and Lucas (1988, 1990).
[12] Södersten (1974e).
[13] Södersten (1991a), Spanish version: Södersten (1990d).

War, the application of Keynesian stabilization measures between the two wars, and the high growth after the Second World War up to 1970. Strangely enough, his account omits the construction of the welfare state. He only touches it *en passant* and hardly even that. This is strange for at least three reasons. In the first place, economic development is usually not defined simply in terms of growth, but the definition as a rule also contains something about a more equal income distribution and abolition of poverty. Secondly, the welfare state was Sweden's claim to international economic and social fame, what was always highlighted in the comparative literature. Finally, during his entire career, Bo had always emphasized distributional aspects—in all kinds of contexts—and then it becomes close to impossible to understand why he—with his Social Democratic heritage—would not emphasize how the fruits of growth had accrued to broad population segments in an account of the construction of modern Sweden.

In an article in Portuguese, on more or less the same theme, published around the same time in the Lisbon journal *Finisterra—Revista de Reflexão e Crítica*, the account is more balanced.[14] In addition to telling the growth story, Bo discusses the political role of the Social Democracy during the same period: the rise of the trade union movement and the Swedish labor market model, the solidarity wage policy, the difference between the export sector and the protected domestic sector, and not least the struggle for equality and income equalization via the tax system.

---

[14] Södersten (1990e).

CHAPTER 10

Three Continents

Bo Södersten's personal experience of developing countries stemmed mainly from Latin America and Africa. Two countries that he kept coming back were Cuba and Chile.

CUBA

Bo first visited Cuba in 1967 and 1968. (Around the same time, he went to Mexico, Costa Rica, and Haiti.) When he returned home, he reported his findings in an article in *Tiden*: the problems connected with the overambitious sugar production target: ten million tons, employment, wages and the lack of consumer goods, the revolutionary enthusiasm, and the government control of the citizens.[1]

Bo was back in Cuba at the beginning of 2000. I was there as well, trying to teach economics to Cuban bureaucrats. Both of us met some Cuban colleagues, and we wrote an article together about the Cuban economy forty years after the revolution.[2] The country was in dire straits. When the Communist regimes collapsed in Eastern Europe, the Cuban GDP took a record dive: between 30 and 50 percent in 1989–1995. Castro was forced

[1] Södersten (1968a).
[2] Lundahl and Södersten (2000).

to permit a limited liberalization of the centrally planned economy, but he lost the historical opportunity and learned nothing from the market economy experience of China and Vietnam. In 2000, Cuba was still a centrally controlled planned economy which displayed the usual signs of failure, not least the humiliating presence of ration books for goods that were nowhere to be seen. The monthly rations lasted a couple of weeks. Castro hated the market economy and the changes that he had allowed had been rolled back as soon as he saw a chance. The everyday life of the ordinary Cuban was dominated by the hunt for daily necessities. The probability that history would absolve Castro was close to zero.

CHILE: ALLENDE AND PINOCHET

Another Latin American country which Bo visited on a few occasions was Chile. The first time was in January 1974, only a few months after the military coup against Salvador Allende. He went there together with the cartoonist EWK (Ewert Karlsson). Bo wrote three articles in *Aftonbladet* where he analyzed Allende's economic policy. He also described the military terror after the coup. Bo got the same eerie feeling as when he visited Papa Doc's Haiti in 1968.[3]

These articles were the starting point for a longer essay, "Socialismen på prov: fallet Chile" ("Socialism on Trial: The Case of Chile"), written with Nancy Barrett from the Urban Institute of the American University in Washington, DC, who had been a visiting professor in Gothenburg in 1973.[4] Nancy and Bo argue that the Allende regime failed to understand the economic situation during his presidency and that it was not familiar with the reform methods of reformist Socialism—an analysis which completely contradicted the prevailing leftist conviction at the time: that what brought Allende down was the intrigues of the right in combination with U.S. imperialism. Allende's economic policy was too ideological and completely unrealistic. The government failed to devise efficient methods for dealing with the economy. The rate of inflation accelerated. Socialization and nationalization did nothing to improve the situation, and the price controls that were introduced led to queues of the Soviet type and black markets. The situation became more and more chaotic and then came the coup. The policies of the Allende government had paved the way for it.

---

[3] Södersten (1974b, 1974c, 1974d).
[4] Published in Södersten (1975).

Ten years later, Bo wrote three more articles on Chile, after another visit to the country.[5] There was no question about the fact that Chile in 1984 was a dictatorship where terror and repression was still present, albeit not on the same scale as during the first years of junta rule. But Chile remained a country of fear and uncertainty. The economy was in bad shape. One of the alleged motives behind the coup had been to rescue the economy. The junta had implemented a neoliberal economic policy: privatization, a minimum of intervention, monetarism, free trade. Inflation had been brought down, production had increased, and goods like fruits and forestry products had begun to be exported.

For a few years, the economy seemed to be recovering and growing. In 1979, however, the Chilean government committed the mistake of tying the peso to the U.S. dollar. When the value of the dollar subsequently increased, Chile experienced export difficulties, while imports increased strongly. The current account of the balance of payments displayed persistent deficits and Chile became one of the most indebted countries in the world. At the same time, open unemployment soared to 25 percent. The gap between the rich and the poor increased.

The year 1984 was a year of uncertainty. The government was hoping for an international upswing. The question was how long it would continue in power. To retire into the barracks was no option. Bo, however, saw some hopeful signs among the opposition: the Christian Democrats and the Socialists. The best economists were found among the former, and the Socialist Party seemed to be overcoming its former inner tensions and was seeking inspiration not in Cuba anymore but in sister parties in democratic European countries like France, Spain, and Greece. This was hopeful in a situation where a sudden collapse of the military regime could not be discarded.

After Bo's 1984 visit, the Chilean economy, which had hit bottom in 1982–1983, entered a growth phase. In 1989, the political situation changed as well. The Pinochet regime lost the elections and was about to be replaced by a democratic coalition government. The following year, Bo visited Chile for the third time and wrote two more newspaper articles which did not endear him to the Swedish left.[6] He pointed out that the Swedish debate about Chile had been ideologically infected and that it was time to wake up to reality. Whatever you might think about the Pinochet

---

[5] Södersten (1984b, 1984c, 1984d).
[6] Södersten (1990f, 1990g).

regime, it had managed to break the dependence on copper, diversify exports and put the economy on a growth path driven by free trade. The democratic coalition had to meet big challenges. The economic policy would not be changed but the new government in addition intended to do something about the large income gaps.

Sweden was preparing financial assistance to Chile. Bo did not think that this was appropriate. The Chilean upper class was enjoying a standard of living which was higher than that of most Swedes and the government simply had to tackle the absurd income distribution. Assistance should only be given during a transition period, as support to the democratization process.

Ten more years would pass before Bo visited Chile for the last time, together with Kristian Nyberg, whose specialty was pension systems. This resulted in a journal article about the Chilean economy 1970–2000. As we have already pointed out, Chile's free trade policy was a long-run success story. The large balance of payments deficits at the beginning of the 1980s were curbed when Chile abandoned the linking of the peso to the dollar and introduced currency controls and a crawling peg system. The peso depreciated, and Chile began to pay off its foreign debt. The positive economic development of the 1980s continued under the democratic regimes of the 1990s and growth began to be translated into the construction of a welfare state. One of the most important components of the latter was a fully funded pension system which had been so successful that it began to serve as a model for other Latin American countries. Altogether, Chile was a country which could look to the future with confidence.[7]

The Chilean experience was vastly superior to the Cuban one.[8] The Swedish press had treated Cuba favorably, while Chile had been portrayed as a country governed by mass murderers. The public opinion was one-eyed. You could, however, not get away from the fact that since Castro had assumed power, 100,000 Cubans had been put in detention camps or in other institutions and between 15,000 and 17,000 had been shot. This had been downplayed in Sweden. The same was true with respect to the incontrovertible economic progress made in Chile, where Allende's failed policies had been replaced by free trade and diversification, while the Cuban economy had broken down after the fall of Communism in Eastern

---

[7] Södersten and Nyberg (2001).
[8] Södersten (2001c).

Europe, and the Cubans had not understood that they had to redirect their economic policy along Chilean lines.

A Latin American country that appealed to Bo was Costa Rica, which he visited in 1967 and 1987. He described it as a country which differed favorably from the other Central American countries. It had avoided rightwing dictatorships and had a democratic left.[9] Bo thought that it was strange that neighboring Sandinist Nicaragua received Swedish foreign aid, but not Costa Rica. Possibly, support to Nicaragua could be motivated by a hope for democratic development, but in that case, it was strange that Costa Rica had received nothing.

Africa

In 1970, Bo got a SIDA assignment to analyze the economies of Botswana and Swaziland and their dependence on South Africa. He spent four weeks in these two countries and produced a report, most of which was reprinted in one of his books of essays.[10] There, he discusses the customs and currency unions with South Africa, which limited the possibility of trading with outside countries and made it difficult to pursue an independent economic policy. Also, workers in the two small countries were dependent on jobs in the South African mining sector. Most people, however, made their living from livestock raising and agriculture, a sector subject to overgrazing. Most Swedish assistance had been concentrated on education, and Bo suggested that this should be continued and expanded.

The second time Bo did development consultancy, he went to Ethiopia as part of a review of the health sector in connection with the country's fourth five-year plan. He participated in the analysis of the costs of the sector. It was clear that the planned expansion of health care could not be financed with the funds allocated in the budget. Either more money would have to be provided or patient fees would have to be introduced.[11]

Bo would also deal with a third country in Southern Africa: Namibia, in 1983, a decade after the Ethiopian study, in a paper presented at a symposium on the economics of the primary sector.[12] At the time, Namibia was administered by South Africa. The country had rich natural resources.

---

[9] Södersten (1984a).
[10] Södersten (1975).
[11] Imperial Ethiopian Government (1973).
[12] Södersten (1985b).

Almost 50 percent of its GDP derived from mineral production. Bo analyzed the Namibian economy in Ricardian terms: more productive (low-cost) mines were exploited before less productive ones. He trusted that the country would become independent in the near future and speculated about how the mineral rents would then be distributed between the state, the capital owners, and the workers. Bo saw a risk that in the process, the rents would be squandered at the expense of future development. Also, Namibia ought to leave the customs union with South Africa in order to speed up the country's industrialization.

Asia

Bo's main first-hand exposure to developing countries stemmed from Latin America and Africa. About Asia he only wrote a few newspaper articles, on Vietnam, India, and Hong Kong. I drafted him for a seminar in Hanoi in 1989 where foreign and Vietnamese economists interacted around the theme of *Doi moi*—fence breaking—the Vietnamese term for liberalization of the economy. In contrast to the Cubans, the Vietnamese had understood that central planning did not work and had introduced the market economy and scrapped central planning and collectivization. Bo saw the results in the streets of Hanoi: goods everywhere—the results of a process that Sweden ought to support.[13]

Another Asian country that had managed the transition from plan to market was India. Bo wrote about it in one of his last articles.[14] After forty years of Soviet thinking about planning, in 1991, the country had changed its course completely and cleaned out the mess of protection and regulations, a measure that put India on a growth path fueled by foreign investment and an excellent education system.

A country with a far gloomier future was Hong Kong, which Bo visited in 1991. It was to be transferred from British to Chinese sovereignty in 1997. Hong Kong had had an amazing growth rate since the 1950s, but what would happen after 1997 was far from clear. The 1989 Tiananmen square massacre had clearly demonstrated what the Chinese Communist

---

[13] Södersten (1989j).
[14] Södersten (2006c).

regime was capable of. About 200,000 people had emigrated from Hong Kong, and it was not in any way clear whether the Communist regime would respect property rights and political freedom in Hong Kong. As we know, it didn't.[15]

---

[15] Södersten (1991d).

CHAPTER 11

In Parliament

In the fall of 1979, Bo began a nine-year period in the Swedish parliament, for the Dalarna constituency. He had been aiming for a political career for quite some time. Bo had a political heritage from home, he had been the chairman of the Social Democratic Laboremus student club for a year during his time in Uppsala. In the 1960s, he had written a number of excellent, ideologically colored essays. During 1971–1972, he had been a regular columnist in *Aftonbladet*.[1] Bo had also lectured, participated in meetings, and spoken on May Day back home in Dalarna, and he saw to it that he was visible in the newspapers by writing on a wide range of subjects: employment, the Swedish exchange rate, growth problems, interest rates, labor-managed firms, the wage-earners' funds, the possibilities of socialism, and so on.

Trying to Make It

Bo was elected, but his years in Parliament did not turn out as he had expected. Being an economics professor, it would have been natural for the party to put him directly into the Standing Committee on Finance, but he had to fight hard to make it there. In 1982, he found that he was

---

[1] He collected most of his columns in Södersten (1975).

"Comrades, participants in the meeting!" Speaking on May Day. (Courtesy Anna Södersten Bengtsson)

the only newly elected Social Democrat MP who was not a permanent member of any parliamentary committee, but just a deputy in the Standing Committee on Taxation. To make it into the Committee on Finance, Bo had to mobilize a number of fellow Social Democrats who would demand it.

Bo remained on the Standing Committee on Finance between 1982 and 1988. In 1983, he also became the chairman on the Government Committee on Capital Gains, whose task was to propose new rules for taxation of shares, bonds, and options. Its work resulted in some minor changes, but the final proposal presented in 1986 was rejected by the Ministry of Finance, a fact which of course mortified Bo a lot. In 1984, more committees on tax issues were appointed, and Bo became member of the Committee on Reformed Income Taxation (Kommittén för reformerad inkomstbeskattning [RINK]).

At the beginning of his years in Parliament, Bo made a serious effort to fall in line with his party. Employment was high on the list of its priorities, and it was important for a new, ambitious MP to defend it. To that end, Bo even went so far as to advocate restrictions on foreign trade.[2] His argu-

---

[2] Södersten (1980b).

ment was that certain countries used illegitimate methods of competition: industrial production which destroyed the environment, bad working conditions, and direct export subsidization, all of which harmed the more ambitious nations. Other countries had resorted to an economic policy which was excessively restrictive and which had harmed Swedish exports. Sweden also had to obtain a reasonable food security, and this called for import restrictions on agricultural goods. Bo's suggestion resulted in a newspaper article by the economist Harry Flam, who lampooned his arguments by quoting his arguments in favor of free trade as he had presented them in *International Economics*.[3]

Bo's economist background made him frequently clash with those of his party colleagues who were more intent on rapid political gains. During a routine Tuesday meeting with all the Social Democratic MPs at the beginning of December 1984, the Minister for Health and Social Affairs, Sten Andersson, argued that the Swedish economy was in such a good shape that it was time to give back to the pensioners what they had lost on the 1982 devaluation. Bo was shocked and said that it was the most stupid thing he had ever heard. When, finally, the economy was beginning to be under control, you could not just start squandering the gains. Andersson was not interested in any discussion of the issue but simply stated that if the party followed Bo's advice, after the next elections, the Social Democratic representation in Parliament might be qualitatively better but quantitatively smaller.[4]

Housing

As we have already seen, Bo's effort did not take him anywhere, so it was only natural that after a while he gave up and began to push his own ideas. One of these, of course, dealt with the housing market. During the 1980s, large subsidies had gone into construction, largely for macroeconomic stabilization reasons. Bo thought that this was a waste of money. The subsidies mainly went to the big cities and not, for example, to his own Dalarna. Bo got in touch with his fellow Social Democratic Dalecarlians for a common motion. The party leadership, however, was completely against it. Bo was admonished first by the leader of the party group and then by the party leader, Ingvar Carlsson. Both failed to

---

[3] Flam (1980).
[4] Södersten (2006b), p. 47.

Bo in the mid-1980s. (Courtesy Anna Södersten Bengtsson)

change his views, but Bo understood that sticking to his guns would put his Dalecarlian fellows in an awkward position and hence withdrew the motion.[5]

The story does, however, not end there. Bo returned with another motion which stated that the subsidies were far too generous, that they tended to contribute to the overheating of the economy, and that the regional focus was mistaken.[6] The housing issue was dealt with in Parliament on 28 April 1988,[7] on a day when many of the MPs, including the Minister of Housing, Hans Gustafsson, were preparing to go home and were listening in their rooms, but when it became clear how hot the topic was, they hurried to the session hall, which was quickly filled, to listen to how Bo did his best to discredit the Social Democratic housing policy.

Of course, nothing came out of Bo's motion, since it was not anchored with the top brass of the party. Looking back on the issue, in 2006, he was,

[5] Ibid., pp. 46–47.
[6] Motion 1987/1988.
[7] Riksdagens protokoll 1987/1988: 110.

however, confident that he had the better arguments. "... history proved that we were right, without any doubt whatsoever. Construction culminated in 1990–91 and then collapsed, which contributed strongly to the depression that set in from the beginning of the 1990s."[8]

The Stumbling Block

Perhaps the most important person in the Social Democratic establishment, as far as Bo was concerned, was Kjell-Olof Feldt, who served as Minister of Finance from 1983 to 1990. Bo and Feldt had met each other during their Uppsala years, but had never become close friends, and had had a few controversies. Bo had told Feldt that he was never going to be anybody. "Bo aspired to become a minister," says Feldt. "When I became Secretary of State in the Ministry of Finance ... he began to show some interest and inquired whether I had any assignment for him, but I didn't find any ... I did not think that Södersten would be a good decision maker. He could drive people nuts with his comments."[9] And he did not know his place in the pecking order. The new Social Democratic MPs were hardly greeted by the old-timers higher-up when they met in the corridors of the parliament building, which of course upset Bo tremendously who, as a university professor, was used to be treated with some respect. But such was the party culture.

According to Feldt, Bo made life in Parliament difficult for himself. He always spoke when economic topics were under discussion. Those discussions were important, since the party group had to arrive at a position, for example, on the budget. In the beginning, many thought that it was great to have a professor of economics in the group, but Bo had a tendency to assume extreme positions. "He went very far with his visions, illusions and aggressions. He easily worked himself up, which was a bit unnecessary in the group discussions. To be an MP turned out to be a disappointment for him, and the more disappointed he got, the more aggressive he turned. He became tougher in the debates. He was simply furious." Bo did not realize that in order to make it in politics you must be able to compromise, listen to others and yield, in order to advance. He was too egocentric, too stubborn and resisted compromises. "He simply became too difficult to control."

[8] Södersten (2006b), p. 48.
[9] Interview with Kjell-Olof Feldt, 21 April 2021.

Bo never managed to anchor his pet project—labor-managed firms—in the party top hierarchy.

> Olof Palme was against the idea. He thought than when the Codetermination in Industry Act had been passed, this was the most important democratic reform since that of universal suffrage. This was what would give the workers influence, not the takeover of firms. It was not possible to go any further without wreaking havoc in Swedish industry. Two philosophies collided, and it was Palme who had the power.[10]

Bo wanted to make a political career, but he had a way of bringing out his own person in a way which made the decision makers who were to assign the MPs political tasks hesitate. He became aggressive against the party group and at times blew his top without any apparent reason. It was difficult to know what had happened. The result was that he never got the positions that he aspired to.

If we are to believe Feldt, this was what made Bo turn around politically. He discovered that the Social Democracy and the parliament offered no career prospects for him. He went from being a radical Social Democrat to becoming a Liberal, in, if not all, at least many respects.

---

[10] Ibid.

CHAPTER 12

The Debater

When Bo Södersten left Parliament in 1988, he returned to his chair in international economics in Lund, where he remained until his retirement in 1996. Two years later, he moved to Jönköping, where his wife, Birgit Friggebo, former Minister of Housing and Culture (including immigration and equality), had become county governor. Bo and Birgit remained there until 2004, when Birgit stepped down. In Jönköping Bo was affiliated to the Jönköping International Business School.

Bo continued writing scientific articles and book chapters and editing books. However, during the rest of his active life, his main activity consisted in writing newspaper articles on (mainly) controversial themes. Bo was a magnificent egocentric, a fact that he was aware of, and which was directly related to his desire to write newspaper articles. "I know that my words will reach many people," he writes in his memoir draft. "Of course, this is nice, since I am an egocentric, but at the same time I want to fight that side by reaching outside myself."[1] The quote does not only convey egocentricity but also the joy of communication. He felt an inner urge to state his view and became obsessed by his theses when he wrote. From 1988, Bo wrote regularly in *Dagens Nyheter*, *Svenska Dagbladet*, *Sydsvenskan*, and *Privata Affärer*, and after moving to Jönköping, also in *Jönköpings-Posten*.

[1] Södersten (2001a).

Birgit and Bo, 1992. (Courtesy Birgit Friggebo)

Some of his articles were republished in collections of essays, but far from all. To *Den hierarkiska välfärden* (*The Hierarchical Welfare*) (1968), which I have already dealt with, have to be added *Den svenska sköldpaddan* (*The Swedish Turtle*) (1975), *Ut ur krisen* (*Out of the Crisis*) (1981), and *Kapitalismen byggde landet* (*Capitalism Built the Country*) (1991).[2] The latter collection, however, only contains articles written between 1984 and 1990 and nothing written between 1991 and 2006 exists in book form. In

[2] Södersten (1968b, 1975, 1981a, 1991l).

Bo's vignette in Sydsvenskan, where he published more than 200 articles between 1988 and 2006

the following, we will make an attempt to deal with Bo's vast article output, roughly arranged by theme.

The first time that Bo became seriously involved in writing newspaper articles was when he wrote chronicles for *Aftonbladet* in 1971–1972, and after 1988, he again picked up this strand. The *Aftonbladet* chronicles dealt mainly with Socialist themes. The Swedish Social Democracy had weathered the crisis of the 1930s and contributed to the survival of capitalism. Wasn't it the time, then, for society to get an influence on how the firms were managed? Wasn't it reasonable that the municipalities should expropriate land without having to pay the owners compensation for value increases that were the result of public measures? Was it reasonable to attempt to realize Socialist goals within a system dominated by capitalism and private property? Did the stock market really contribute to capital formation, or should it be compared with betting on the ponies? Bo wrote in *Aftonbladet* about the distribution of income between labor and capital, he criticized the political parties—right and left—he reviewed books, not least the memoirs of Bertil Ohlin, and in a comment of the new edition of Myrdal's classic *Vetenskap och politik i nationalekonomin* (*The Political Element in the Development of Economic Theory*) from 1972,[3] he criticized

---

[3] Myrdal (1972). The English translation is from 1953 (Myrdal 1953).

Myrdal for not including his teacher Gustav Cassel among the economists that posed as scientists when they acted as politicians.

More essays

Economic Policy

Bo Södersten frequently participated in the debate on Swedish economic policy during his entire professional career. We have already dealt with some such instances. Here are some more. They show how his views changed over time, as a result of his movement from the left to the right on the political scale when he left Parliament in 1988. In his youth, he was an ardent Socialist who advocated extensive intervention in the market mechanism and a large public sector. During his Parliament years, however, he gradually became convinced that excessive tampering with the market might result in various types of government failure and reduced welfare.

In 1971, Bo commented the budget of the Social Democrats. It stressed industrial investment. The private companies had been granted a 10 percent deduction on their investments, but Bo argued that these investments should be controlled by the state as part of the creation of a planned economy.[4]

In 1976, Sweden got its first non-Socialist government since the 1930s. When it had been in power for a year, Bo reviewed its economic policy.[5] The krona had been devalued twice, which of course should have a positive effect on exports and dampen imports. Devaluation, however, was essentially a short-run measure which mainly served to give the economy breathing space and its efficiency was dependent of whether the overall demand could be restricted, and the new government had not managed to do that. In order to ensure a long-run expansion of the economy, completely different measures were called for. The solution—as always for Bo at that time—was found in a combination of labor-managed firms and wage-earners' funds.

In 1981, Bo Södersten published his third collection of essays, *Ut ur krisen* (*Out of the Crisis*).[6] The title essay analyzes the 1970s' crisis and the crisis policy of the Liberal-Center-Conservative government. Bo argued that it had failed. The government had succeeded in reducing the cost level, which had resulted in wage reductions. The stimulation measures set in in 1978 and 1979 had led to an increase of the size of the public sector, while the effects on the private sector had been small, and the income distribution had been become more unequal. Bo called the tax cuts that had been introduced reactionary.

Bo sketched an alternative economic policy. The current account of the balance of payments was negative so he wanted to switch the demand from imported to domestic goods. A devaluation would presumably lead to increased inflation. Bo wanted to stimulate the supply instead, via selective measures directed at specific branches, like import substitution in the energy sector. The nuclear power issue was locked after the 1980 referendum (see below), but Bo wanted to de-ideologize it and let the economic arguments speak. Another such measure was subsidization of the construction of dwellings.

---

[4] Södersten (1971a).
[5] Södersten (1977c).
[6] Södersten (1981a).

In 1982, the Social Democrats were back in power. Sweden received some help from abroad—the United States and West Germany, but an OECD forecast for 1986 indicated that the Swedish growth rate might deviate negatively from that of the rest of the Western world. Hence, a growth-oriented economic policy was needed.[7] The question was what would happen to the Swedish standard of living in the longer run.[8] Bo saw three threats. The first was our international dependence. Unless Sweden was at the front of technical development, factor prices would be equalized and wages would be reduced. The second was the increased foreign debt. This had increased from 70 billion kronor in 1976 to 350 billion in 1982, and it was possible that all the fruits of growth, and more, might have to be spent on servicing this. The third problem was that the trade unions had developed into special interest groups which made demands that were not compatible with the growth rate. The public interest had to be strengthened at the expense of union and other special interests. Bo hoped that the Social Democrats would be rational enough to realize this.

In this situation, Conservative criticism might have a role to play. Surprisingly, Bo stated that the Swedish Social Democracy would benefit from a Conservative slave on the triumphal chariot.[9] No other Western industrial nation had such a weak bourgeoisie as Sweden, but this did not mean that it had no role to play. The Conservative tradition of ideas had played an important role in the Swedish industrialization process—hard work, altruism, and imagination. It would therefore be good for the Social Democrats to sharpen their claws against Conservative criticism. The Conservatives, however, had not managed and developed their heritage but had degenerated into the defense of privileges, grumbling, and flight from reality. The heritage—the good tradition—had to be resurrected.

Sweden's comparative situation was not good. We were on our way down from the welfare peak. Stagnation had been substituted for one hundred years of brilliant growth. Sweden was sliding downward in the welfare league. The productivity of the public sector displayed a downward trend, while at the same time the sector was growing.[10]

[7] Södersten (1985d).
[8] Södersten (1985c).
[9] Södersten (1986).
[10] Södersten (1987c).

The year 1988 was Bo Södersten's last year in Parliament. Toward the end of it he concluded that the Social Democrats had managed the economic policy relatively well. Above all, they had managed to reduce both the public expenditures and the budget deficits. Bo called for further expenditure reductions, but the parliamentary situation, with the Greens tipping the scales, made this difficult. Bo wanted agreements across party lines. It was time to say goodbye to bloc politics and be pragmatic.[11]

Before the 1988 parliamentary elections, the political scientist Leif Lewin had published the book *Det gemensamma bästa* (*The Common Good*), where he contended that the voters were not driven by egoism but by far nobler motives, the common interest.[12] Bo disagreed. In Sweden, the public interest had problems asserting itself against egoism. It was easy to find examples: wage bargaining, the agricultural policy, which was dominated by the producers, and housing, where the construction industry, the cooperative housing movement, and the tenants' association in different ways pushed their own interests and none of the political parties had shown any interest in changing the situation.[13]

* * *

Leaving Parliament put Bo Södersten in more or less the same frustrating situation as the one he was in in the mid-1960s. Hans O. Sjöström reflected on it:

> Södersten served ... as a kind of an ideological beacon for us younger Laboremites. Thereby, he contributed to the recruitment of younger and later very useful recruits for the various levels of the administration. But the party has neglected to use this talent of his. He does not play any prominent role in Parliament, he will certainly not become a cabinet minister and he has not been able to make use of his position as a professor to become a heavyweight voice in the political debate in the country.[14]

The above constitutes an adequate summary of position of Bo Södersten when he left Parliament—a summary which provides a background to his ideological development during the following decade.

[11] Södersten (1988b).
[12] Lewin (1988).
[13] Södersten (1988c).
[14] Sjöström (1987), pp. 85–86.

CHAPTER 13

Saulus Falls off the Horse

In 1990, Bo launched his frontal attack on the Social Democrats. In an article in *Dagens Nyheter* with the provocative title "Kapitalismen byggde landet" ("Capitalism Built the Country"),[1] an article which also provided the title of his last book of essays,[2] he contended that the Social Democrats had played a very small role in the process that created Sweden's wealth. The 1989 variety of the party did not live any life of its own. It was in a complete symbiosis with capitalism and that had been the case for very long. And it was capitalism that had been leading with the Social Democracy following. Without the capitalistic market economy, the Social Democracy would not have had any role to play.

Bo brought out a perspective that he had used on many occasions, that of the Swedish high and even growth between 1870 and 1970. This was not due to the Social Democrats but exclusively thanks to private capitalism, which had collaborated with the state long before the Social Democracy had become a power factor to reckon with. Not even during the 1930s had it played any decisive role. What put a brake on the depression in Sweden was that we abandoned the gold standard, but that was in

---

[1] Södersten (1990j).
[2] Södersten (1991l).

The turnaround

1931, the year before the Social Democrats formed their government, and the rate of unemployment stayed at the 10 percent level throughout the decade. The "miracle years" of the 1950s and 1960s, in turn, were due to the international boom.

The role of the Social Democrats had simply been that of the distributor. The party redistributed the wealth crated by the capitalist growth process, but it had never understood its actual role. "The lack of ideological insight and the lack of history which characterizes several leading Social Democrats is ... tragic, with its complete ridiculousness and will doubtlessly influence ... our domestic policy negatively."[3]

The year before the parliamentary elections in 1991, Bo wrote an article where he criticized the Social Democratic crisis package.[4] Too many remained outside the labor market, and it was too easy to manipulate the system of social insurance. The Swedish krona was under pressure, the package was not focused and nothing was done to address the structural problems. The Social Democrats risked losing the elections, which was precisely what happened.

[3] Södersten (1990j).
[4] Södersten (1990l).

A New Government

In another article, written after the elections, Bo reflected about what could happen after the "historical" loss when the long leftist trend in Swedish politics was broken. The Social Democrats and the Left received less than 43 percent of the votes, the Greens were thrown out of Parliament, and two new parties entered: the Christian Democrats and New Democracy, both on the right. Bo was not certain that the Social Democrats were prepared to undertake any self-examination. They behaved like the proverbial ostrich, arguing that they did better than what could be expected from the poll results, an interpretation that was certain to be accepted by the majority of their members.[5]

Bo was not terribly impressed by the new government. The new Prime Minister, Carl Bildt, had managed to put the wrong people in the wrong positions. Bo thought that the government was falling apart. It consisted of too many weak links.[6] The bourgeois parties had problems with the public sector. Each party concentrated on its pet questions and failed to see the overall picture. The public sector was too large and too unproductive. The low-productive parts had to be trimmed and the ATP pension system (see below) had to be phased out in favor of a fully funded system. Bo suggested the creation of a few committees to look into the different problems. The new government lacked reform ideas. What was needed was an unprejudiced retreat from exaggerated and unrealistic welfare ambitions. Marginal adjustments would not do. The government could not continue to focus on the traditional recipients and favor its own voters.[7]

The year 1994 was both an election year and the year when the Swedish people was to vote about a possible entry into the EG. The best thing would be if after the elections the Social Democrats and the Moderates could cooperate. The smaller parties had demonstrated their negative impact on the economic policy. If the Greens made it back into Parliament, they were likely to collaborate with the Left and turn the Social Democrats in the populist direction, with uncontrolled budget deficits and possibly a no to the EG.[8]

---

[5] Södersten (1991i).
[6] Södersten (1992g).
[7] Södersten (1992h, 1992i).
[8] Södersten (1994e).

Back in Power

The elections resulted in a safe leftist majority. The Social Democrats were back in government. Bo thought that a majority of the Swedish people wanted a government with both Social Democrats and Conservatives, but that was impossible. Party politics was about power, and the gap between the Social Democrats and the Moderates was unbridgeable. The only alternative was a Social Democratic government, an alternative that did not appeal to Bo. A difficult economic and political winter was coming up.[9]

A fortnight later, Bo sharpened his tone against the Left. How much was its triumph in the elections worth? Its analysis of the causes of the economic crisis was erroneous—the 1990 tax reform and the deregulations of the credit and currency markets had created a speculation economy and a bank crisis, and unemployment was due to the low total demand. The parties on the left had problems making it beyond the traditional Keynesian recipe. But the situation required control of the budget deficit, not expansion. The Greens and the Left probably wanted to go back to the old regulations but that was impossible.[10]

On the left, the skepticism against the market economy was cemented. It made leftist policies impossible, it was undemocratic, and it made it impossible to arrive at a reasonable income distribution. Bo thought that this position was hilarious.[11] There was no such thing as the "right" income distribution. Voting would result in majority exploitation of the minority. The economic sphere had to be separated from the political one. The opulence of the Western world rested on the fact that arbitrary political interventions in the economy had been ruled out. As Bo saw it, the Swedish problem was not that markets had been given free reign. On the contrary, the political system had to take a step back and let the market work on its own premises.

Bo saw a flight from reality among the Swedish politicians. The media were chasing sensations and entertainment and the politicians loved to sit down in the TV sofas. Neither the politicians nor the media had the stamina to focus long on the problems, even when they had long-term implications. Pseudo problems were invented that were substituted for the real ones.[12]

---

[9] Södersten (1994g).
[10] Södersten (1994h).
[11] Södersten (1995d).
[12] Södersten (1994i).

In 1997, the Social Democrats had one year left in office. Bo did not think that they had managed the economic policy particularly well. Unemployment was high, which was due not least to the mistrust of the market. The party preferred state monopolies and an expansion of the public sector. This had resulted in a high tax burden and low growth and employment.[13]

Left Turn

During the next elections, in 1998, the Social Democrats lost 30 seats, whereas the Left won 21. This did not bode well. The former would have to lean on the latter, with all that this implied in terms of populism and hostility against the market. More monopolies and subsidies of the public sector were sure to come. The Prime Minister, Göran Persson, had not been able to resist and had therefore lost authority.[14]

In 1999, Bo pointed out that Sweden was particularly sensitive to changes in the international economy because of its large public sector and its high tax burden. The country had failed to put the economy in order during the upswing in the 1980s, in bright contrast to countries like Holland and Denmark. The necessary measures had to be implemented during good times, not bad. If not, the situation would simply grow worse. The contrast between Holland and Denmark, on the one hand, and Sweden, on the other, was bright. Sweden had ended up in a situation of political passivity, high unemployment, and dependency on social insurance, while Holland and Denmark had addressed the problem and cut the unemployment rate in half. The rate of growth of the economies of the latter two countries had been twice as high as the Swedish one.[15]

Jobless Growth

In August 2005, Erik Jonasson, Lars Pettersson, and Bo criticized the Swedish employment policy.[16] At the beginning of the 1990s, the labor market had been subject to the biggest shock since the 1930s. Half a million jobs disappeared. Between 1994 and 1998, the economy was "cleaned

---

[13] Södersten (1997d).
[14] Södersten (1998e).
[15] Södersten (1999d).
[16] Jonasson et al. (2005).

up," but in the wrong way: by increasing the tax burden. No less than 85 percent of the GDP increase 1994–2000 was taxed away. In 2005, unemployment remained high so the government put together a work group which would suggest how the labor supply could be increased. Erik, Lars, and Bo argued that this amounted to putting the cart before the horse. Never, in modern times, had so many been outside the labor market. Instead, the demand for labor must be stimulated, and the expansion had to take place in the private, competitive sector, through tax reductions.

The growth rate of the Swedish economy was decent: 2.3 percent per annum, but employment did not expand any longer. Far too many were outside the labor force and far too many, especially in Norrland, were reported sick, for reasons that were not exclusively medical. Sweden was not doing as well as the majority might believe.[17] Why were there no new jobs? In economies at the level of development of Sweden, most new employment opportunities were created in the service sectors. The demand for childcare and care of the elderly, education, travel, and entertainment increased with income. Sweden had opted for producing many of these services in the public sector. The latter was bloated and its productivity was low. The competitive sectors, in turn, were capital-intensive and their growth did not create many jobs. The employment opportunities were found in the service sectors, but these had to be exposed to competition and their production had to be determined by the market.

---

[17] Södersten (2005e).

CHAPTER 14

The Overgrown Public Sector

It was inevitable that Bo would deal with the public sector. During his Socialist period, he defended it, like when in 1971, he began a polemic about how SACO (the Swedish Confederation of Professional Associations) calculated real wages. SACO had concentrated exclusively on private consumption by calculating the after-tax wage. The taxes paid by its members were wasted and increases of the contributions to social insurance could only lead to a reduced living standard. Bo thought that it was sensational that an organization where the majority of the members were producing public services would completely disregard the utility of its own work.[1]

Lars Tobisson, the SACO head of investigations, answered that Bo's accusation was blatantly wrong. The organization had never denied the welfare value of public services, but its members as a rule paid more in taxes that what they got back, and the after-tax wage was more interesting than the pre-tax wage as far as the private consumption standard was concerned.[2]

[1] Södersten (1971b).
[2] Tobisson (1971).

Taxes

In connection with his participation in the committees on capital gains and reformed income taxation in the 1980s, Bo edited a book on the new tax system that was being forged, *Skattereform och skatteplanering* (*Tax Reform and Tax Planning*).[3] The proposal was not finished when the book was published, and it was not certain whether it would receive support in Parliament. Nevertheless, Bo considered it important that the general public should get a view of the existing alternatives and the reasoning behind the reform work.

Bo's own chapter dealt with the probable effects of a broadened tax base and changes in capital taxation.[4] He discussed not only the technical aspects but also the political factors that influenced the work. One of the most important proposals was a lowering of the tax on labor incomes, a measure applauded by the center-right parties but booed by the Left and the Greens. The Social Democrats had supported the committee work but all their members might not agree.

The year after the publication of *Skattereform och skatteplanering*, Bo edited a second volume on the same theme, *Den stora reformen* (*The Great Reform*).[5] By then, the proposal had been worked out, and it was passed in Parliament in December 1990. It implied that 90 percent of all Swedish taxpayers would pay only local taxes and not state income tax. The lower limit for the latter in the end was fixed at 180,000 kronor, an agreement which became known as "the tax reform of the century." Bo's own introductory chapter is basically a variation on the theme he presented in the first book. He accounts for how the reform was conceived and presents its probable economic effects.

Nourishing and Draining

Taxes are but one component of the public sector. Another important aspect of the latter was its size, the largest among the industrialized market economies. Bo thought that it had grown *too* large, and its productivity was low, which was reflected in the wage level. The remedy was obvious.

---

[3] Södersten (1989a).
[4] Södersten (1989b)
[5] Södersten (1990b).

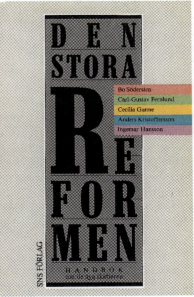

The need for tax reform

The productivity of the public sector could only be increased through stimulation of the employees and a reduction of their number. This should not be too difficult. Labor was scarce in Sweden at the end of the 1980s, so people did not risk becoming unemployed.[6] This would, however, soon change. At the beginning of the 1990s, Sweden entered a period of economic stagnation. By then, it was difficult to find mechanisms which made it possible to move people out of an ever more inefficient public sector into the more productive parts of the economy.[7]

In 1992, Bo Södersten assumed a more and more aggressive position vis-à-vis the public sector. He did not hesitate to call it "draining (tärande)" as opposed to the "nourishing" private sector. In two articles in *Dagens Nyheter* at the end of the year, he contended that those who were looking for the roots of Sweden's economic problems were

---

[6] Södersten (1988d).
[7] Södersten (1991j).

looking in the wrong place. He presented a table showing how the balance between the "nourishing" and "draining" sectors had changed between 1970 and 1992. Among the latter, he included those in the public sector, the pensioners, those reported sick and on parental leave, those seeking asylum, those in the programs of the National Labour Market Board, and the openly unemployed. The former were those employed in the private sector. The ratio of "draining" to "nourishing"' had increased from 0.9 in 1970 to almost 2.3 in 1992. The former group was paid through taxes and contributions. The number of nourishing had been reduced while the number of employees in the public sector had increased. This was no sound development, since the productivity in the latter sector had deceased. In addition, many had opted out of the labor market. The real age of retirement had decreased from 67 to 61–62 thanks to generous rules and high compensation levels.[8] The "central Swedish problem" was how to restore the balance between the two groups.

In common parlance, the shit hit the fan. The politically correct and the employees objected to Bo's vocabulary. He was depicted as a vulgar agitator, declaring the employees in the public sector parasites, a humbug, and a categoric economic guru, who by his writings hardly contributed anything "nourishing."[9] However, Bo thought he was right. "From the first journey abroad, the consumption of the public employees and their clients is paid with tax money from the private sector."[10] The welfare state belonged to the past. Jobs were lost in the industrial sector and people on welfare had been substituted for workers. Those in the public sector did not have to contribute to their wages. The taxpayers saw to it that they got paid.[11] Bo thought that the policy built on the "After us the deluge" principle.[12]

[8] Södersten (1992d, 1992e).
[9] Sundell (1993), Bergqvist (1993). See also Rothstein and Boëthius (1993).
[10] Södersten (1993c).
[11] Södersten (1993d).
[12] Södersten (1993f).

14 THE OVERGROWN PUBLIC SECTOR

"You have to understand ..."

The attacks on Bo's vocabulary continued, and Bo continued his attacks on the overdimensioned public sector for several years. In 1994, Bengt Furåker, professor of sociology in Gothenburg, contended that his writings sprang from his antipathies against the public sector.[13] His vocabulary was unfortunate, and his statistics were shaky. The dependency ratio must be calculated on the basis of the entire population. Those paid for by the private sector amounted to no more than 32 percent in 1992, and the figure was shrinking, a picture that differed radically from the one presented by Bo.

---

[13] Furåker (1994).

Bo, however, continued his criticism in 1994. Sweden had 600,000 openly unemployed or in public employment programs and a budget deficit that was matched only by that of Greece.[14] It could be reduced only through public sector reforms: pensions, family policy, and a reduction of the exaggerated payments via the social security system.[15] The reform of the public sector was not simply a matter of cutting back[16] but also of reprioritization: in the industrial sector and in education, to ensure that people would work in high-productivity branches.[17] But the politicians stood out as powerless and did nothing.

Pensions: The Reform of the ATP System

One of the most important components of the public sector is pensions. At the beginning of the 1990s, the public sector was handling more than 60 percent of Sweden's resources. In spite of this stunning fact, no textbooks existed which dealt with it. Bo therefore edited an anthology where he contributed a chapter on pensions himself.[18] The chapter is mainly a historical account of how Sweden got a pay-as-you-go system where current payments financed the expenditures during the same year, a fact which Bo attributes to the strong economic growth 1870–1960.[19] He then discusses the differences between this and a fully funded system, where the individuals' pensions are based on their previous payments. In the Swedish ATP supplementary pension system this link was missing, which might lead to problems in the future, if current savings declined.

Bo thought that the Swedish pension system had defects, but a transition to a fully funded system was not without problems either. The members of the generation which had to pay for the phase-out of the pay-as-you-go system without getting any pensions within this system themselves would in principle pay their pensions twice, both in the old system and in the new, fully funded, one.

---

[14] Södersten (1994b).
[15] Södersten (1994c).
[16] Södersten (1994d).
[17] Södersten (1994f).
[18] Södersten (1992b).
[19] Södersten (1992c).

14 THE OVERGROWN PUBLIC SECTOR

Problems of the public sector

Changes of the ATP system were on their way. In 1993, a work group in the Ministry for Social Affairs was working on a reform scheduled for 1994, one which would establish a link between lifetime incomes and pensions. Bo thought that this was an indication of a "limited sobering up" and pointed to the absurdities of the actual system, for example, that pensions were calculated only on the income of the fifteen best years and you had to work for a mere thirty years to get full pension: a system where low-wage earners who had worked their entire adult lives had to subsidize high-income earners with short careers.[20]

In 1994, the pension system was changed into a system based on payments. Bo was worried about the financial aspects. The tax burden was so high that it was doubtful whether the taxpayers could stand any more taxes and fees. Half the pension fees would be paid by the employers and the other half by the employees themselves, which would increase the average tax rate to 60 percent and the marginal one to 75–80 percent.[21]

---

[20] Södersten (1993g).
[21] Södersten (1995f). For an evaluation of the 1994 pension reform, see Kruse and Ståhlberg (2020).

The work on the pension reform continued after 1994. The reform was not sanctioned until 1998. One feature of the reformed system was that the individuals themselves could determine how 2.5 percent of the payments would be placed. However, in 1999, this was being sabotaged by the state, argued Bo, by confiscating up to 90 percent the fee agreed between the individual and the institution he had contracted to handle his funds, which would make the transaction unprofitable for the private agents.[22]

Bo wanted to see a fully funded system where the size of the pensions was determined exclusively by what the individuals had paid and of how well their funds were administered. Good institutions had an important role to play. The pension system had to be removed from the political sphere and transferred to the exclusively economic one.[23]

---

[22] Södersten (1999b).
[23] Södersten (1991j).

CHAPTER 15

Nuclear Power, Childcare, and Higher Education

Nuclear Power

In 1980, the future of nuclear power was subjected to a referendum in Sweden. Bo belonged to the so-called Line 2, which was in favor of a gradual phase-out, determined by how much electricity the country needed to preserve employment and welfare. When, at the end of the 1980s, the question of an early phase-out (no more than ten years) was put on the political agenda, Bo argued that this amounted to economic madness. Nuclear power was cheap and efficient, and a premature phase-out would lead to large economic losses. No realistic possibility existed that alternative, sustainable energy sources could be substituted for it in the short run. Sweden needed nuclear power for its future development.[1]

In 1990, when it had been decided that the twelve existing Swedish nuclear reactors should be closed, on grounds that Bo thought completely erroneous, he edited an anthology where he and eight other authors defended the use of nuclear power.[2] It dealt with the relative costs of nuclear and other forms of power, the economic implications of a phase-out, and the issue of pricing and consumption of electricity.

---

[1] Södersten (1989f, 1989g, 1990k).
[2] Södersten (1990c).

In defense of nuclear power

Sweden had a strong comparative advantage in electricity production, not only hydroelectric power but also nuclear power. The Swedish politicians, however, wanted to destroy the latter, an attitude that indicated not only lack of contact with reality but also fishing for votes.[3] When, in 1997, it was decided that the Barsebäck power station would be closed, Bo reacted immediately and called the decision irrational.[4]

In 1999, it was time again. Twenty years had passed since the referendum, and Bo thought that the Swedish energy policy still was as bizarre as then. It was not possible to scrap nuclear power and simultaneously cut down on the use of fossil fuels. If you did not want the former, the natural thing was to import electricity and increase the use of natural gas.[5] Bo could never let go of the idea that the Swedish attitude to nuclear power was irrational. In 2004, he thought that it was time to wake up and reconsider the nuclear power decision. Why not use the fact that Sweden had one of the most efficient power systems in the world: combined hydroelectric and nuclear power. The latter had contributed to the success of Swedish industry, but the Social Democrats were undecided.[6]

[3] Södersten (1996g).
[4] Södersten (1997c).
[5] Södersten (1999c).
[6] Södersten (2004e).

Daycare Centers or Preschools?

Somewhat unexpectedly, Bo Södersten entered the debate about family policy and public childcare which had been initiated by Alva and Gunnar Myrdal in their book *Kris i befolkningsfrågan* (*Crisis in the Population Question*) from 1934, where they advocated collective childcare and daycare centers in order to make it possible for women to enter the labor market.[7] Bo did not agree. He thought that the Swedish family policy had derailed.[8] In 1981, he had been a member of a group from the Swedish parliament which had made a study trip to Leipzig and Paris to study childcare methods there. The conclusion of the trip was that the Swedish system was inefficient and costly, had far more personnel than needed, and lacked an elaborate pedagogic structure.[9]

Instead of the daycare centers, Bo advocated a voluntary preschool from the age of three, with a pedagogy that made it possible for a single teacher to handle twelve to fifteen children, which was impossible within the daycare center structure. This would free resources that would make it possible to take care of the children also before and after their school hours. Bo had brought the issue up in Parliament for the first time in a motion in 1984 and continued to do so during the rest of his period there.[10] In Lund, an experiment along the lines suggested by Bo was going on, at the Arken preschool, which indicated that it was possible for two preschool teachers to handle between fifteen and twenty children. Bo thought it worthwhile to extend the experiment but the local "daycare center Stalinists," the politicians from the governing coalition, the Social Democrats, the Left Party-the Communists, and the Green Party, together with the daycare personnel, did their best to put an end to it.[11]

Nothing happened, however, and Bo thought that the Swedish childcare system was hopeless. Sweden was a high-tax country, but the Swedes were not free to choose. Couples that wanted to raise their children at home—not leave them in daycare centers—received no contributions whatsoever. Bo thought it immoral to deprive the citizens of 65 percent of their incomes and then not let them choose themselves.[12]

---

[7] Myrdal and Myrdal (1934).
[8] Södersten (1988a).
[9] Fransson et al. (1981).
[10] Södersten (2006b), pp. 36–37.
[11] Södersten (1989h, 1989i).
[12] Södersten (1996f).

University Politics

Between 1990 and 1966, Bo Södersten was the chairman of the Swedish Association of University Teachers—SULF. When he began, the universities were administered by the state, centrally administered. However, the view of central control had begun to change. Decentralization, autonomy, and foundation colleges began to be prestige words in academic circles.

Bo was worried about the quality of the universities. They had to be reformed. He had taken a strong position on the issue in a 1987 article: "Ryck upp universiteten!" ("Upgrade the Universities!").[13] The universities had a distinctive character that had to be preserved. They could not be centrally managed, but the departments had to have a high degree of autonomy. The incentive structure had to be functional. The recruitment to university position had to be based on scientific merits—on the tenure track system—but the reality was different. Too many people saw university positions simply as a way of making a living, had been appointed on obscure criteria, and had no interest in developing scientifically. Also, the bureaucratic garbage had to be removed. "The universities are not there for all kinds of administration. Research and teaching are their only central tasks."[14]

The universities had been mistreated and starved for twenty years, and the definition of what was a university education was very generous indeed. The idea seemed to be to keep the Swedish youths away from the universities and give them a more "practical" education, an idea that had met with success. The universities were under-dimensioned and half the teaching staff lacked a PhD. This was fatal in the long run.[15]

In 1991, Bo presented a proposal for reform of the Swedish university system.[16] It needed more resources but also increased efficiency. Central control had to go. The universities could handle the admission system themselves, based on marks and tests and such grotesque rules as the 25:4 paragraph had to be abolished. A person who was twenty-five and had worked for four years could himself determine that he could enter non-restricted courses. It was not reasonable that first-year students with no overview of the university system and administrative and technical

---

[13] Södersten (1987b).
[14] Ibid.
[15] Södersten (1990m).
[16] Södersten (1991h).

personnel should make decisions about scientific issues. Those who possessed the factual knowledge should also govern the departments and universities.

In 1992, Bo edited a debate anthology, *Pendeln svänger—röster i högskoledebatten* (*The Pendulum Swings—Voices in the University Debate*) with contributions from politicians, administrators, and academics who got an opportunity to present their views.[17] The pendulum had begun to swing back from the centralized extreme and this called for analysis and debate. Bo stressed that Sweden's opulence built on knowledge and that knowledge built on education. The competence of the high-school teachers had to be increased and assistant lectureships and lectureships should be abolished since they offered no opportunity for research. All academic teachers should both do research and teach.

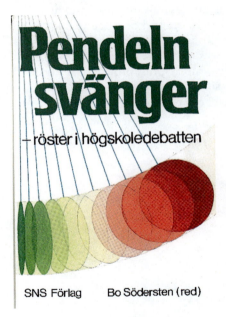

University politics

---

[17] Södersten (1992a).

Another problem was the lack of female representation among higher academic positions. When in 1994, the Minister of Education, Carl Tham, declared that this had to be changed, Bo and SULF produced a concrete program of action. Women who applied and qualified for a professorship but were not ranked first should be given their own chairs. Special support should also be provided on the road toward a possible professorship. All this required money and it was the duty of the ministry to provide it.[18]

Bo did not drop the university issues after stepping down as chairman of SULF. In 2004, he pointed out that the quality of the Swedish universities was about to be undermined. The quality requirements on doctoral dissertations had been lowered and chairs were manned by internal recruitment and promotion instead of by advertisement and open competition. Outside customers should not determine the contents of research. That would turn the universities into simple consultancy firms. The universities had to be led by professors and other academic researchers and teachers. The university world had to be viewed in a wider perspective. Sweden's economic success was to a large extent built on the principle of meritocracy, but in certain contexts, this principle had been discarded, like when at Uppsala University admission to law studies had been based on ethnic criteria instead of school grades.[19]

---

[18] Jalakas (1994).
[19] Södersten (2004f).

CHAPTER 16

Two Controversial Issues

Immigration

One of the most controversial questions within the European Union was immigration. Sweden's policy had deviated considerably from that of more restrictive countries, like Finland.[1] It worked until 1970: labor immigration which yielded a net contribution to GDP. Thereafter, however, the picture had changed, with the immigration of refugees. The immigrants were heavily overrepresented among those on welfare, and they had problems making it into the Swedish labor market. The integration process worked best in smaller places with industry jobs. In the big cities, notably Stockholm, Gothenburg, and Malmö, the situation was worse. The integration there was miserable. Bo posed the question whether the immigration policy should not be changed so as to favor well-educated groups from Eastern Europe.

Bo and three other economists compared the Swedish immigration policy with the Danish one. The Swedish share of immigrants of the total population was twice the Danish one. In Denmark, seven years of residence was required for a permanent residence permit, persons who had committed crimes were deported immediately, the immigration of family members was limited, and the immigrants had to prove that they could

---

[1] Södersten (2001b).

support themselves. In Sweden, where requirements were less stringent, the immigrants had problems in the labor market. The simple manual jobs had disappeared, and in certain groups, open unemployment was as high as 40–50 percent. What would the situation for the second-generation immigrants be like? Would they share the alienation of the first generation? And what would the political consequences be? Would the tougher Danish attitude spread to Sweden?[2]

Bo thought that the Swedish immigration policy had been a mess for twenty years.[3] Integration had failed, and the net cost of immigration amounted to 2–3 percent of GDP. As Bo put it, this meant that many immigrant groups did not work but lived on welfare. Among African and Arab males, the rate of employment was below 50 percent, and among women a great deal less. Around 80 percent of those applying for asylum lacked identification papers, an indication that they wanted to hide something for the authorities.

The Swedish Prime Minister, Göran Persson, appeared not to share Bo's views on labor immigration. He had cautioned against "social tourism" from the new EU countries, which Bo interpreted as resistance to labor immigration from the Baltic states and Poland.[4] Sweden had signed the Maastricht treaty, with its four liberties, one of which was labor mobility, and hence could not pursue the opposite policy.

> It seems to me ... as if Swedish immigration policy more and more is becoming a piece of absurd theater. There is a risk that the workers who want to come here and who can support themselves and who we need so well will be excluded. At the same time, ever more refugees who will live on welfare will try to come here. In a situation where the Swedish welfare state is about to crackle this position is hardly tenable anymore.[5]

A city which had been hit hard by the inability of the immigrants to support themselves was Malmö, where the employment situation was much worse than in other comparable cities. One reason for this was the high share of immigrants in the population, 24 percent, and their high dependence on welfare. The Social Democratic political strongman in Malmö, Ilmar Reepalu, had demanded a change, and his colleague in

---

[2] Ekberg et al. (2002).
[3] Södersten (2003a).
[4] Ibid.
[5] Ibid. For a critique of Bo's statement, see Ekdal (2003).

Gothenburg, Göran Johansson, shared his views, but to no avail. The government had simply offered more welfare contributions.[6]

Bo indefatigably continued his campaign. Certain immigrant groups systematically abused the welfare system: people born in Greece and Turkey and women born, for example, in Lebanon and Syria. Every second male born in Greece in the fifty-to-fifty-nine age group, 43 percent of the women between forty and forty-nine, and 85 percent in the sixty-to-sixty-four interval had been granted early retirement and so had every third male and female aged fifty to fifty-nine from Turkey and former Yugoslavia. Bo's figures had been fetched from an official inquiry. However, strangely enough, the inquiry was being phased out. All the Swedish members of the inquiry committee had been sacked, and Mona Sahlin, the Minister of Integration, had appointed a new commission, led by a person with immigrant background, Masoud Kamali. "Minister Mona Sahlin appears to contend that native Swedes should not or are not fit to do research on immigration issues," thundered Bo.[7]

It was obvious that the Swedish social policy must be redirected toward more self-support and less welfare. Early retirement alone cost 50 billion kronor per year, which Bo thought was an absurdly high figure, and nobody knew on what grounds it was granted. It could not be made dependent on the lifestyle chosen by individuals or families or on arbitrary decisions made by local social insurance offices led by local politicians who had responsibility for their economic activities.

More Welfare Abuse: "The Catching Culture"

The Swedish employment policy contributed to job creation until the beginning of the 1990s. Then, however, Sweden entered a crisis. The level of employment was reduced both for men and women. Sweden had failed to reform the economy and, according to Bo, had become a "workfare state," a state which increased employment through generous financial contributions and by an equally generous social policy that made it possible to retire early. At the same time, the wage policy obstructed the transfer of labor from the low-productive public sector to the high-productive private sector, notably the export sector. The solidarity wage policy in combination with the feminist ideology which demanded special wage

---

[6] Södersten (2004c).
[7] Södersten (2004d). For a retrospective view, see Widmalm (2019).

increases for women made wages increasingly equal. All this led to the creation of negative attitudes in the labor market, attitudes which, however, changed when unemployment soared in the 1990s and the public finances deteriorated and with them the sickness absence benefits. People went back to the labor market. For Bo, it was obvious that the Swedish welfare state was in trouble. It had been allowed to grow in an uncontrolled manner and in the wrong direction.[8]

Between 1994 and 2004, Sweden's GDP had grown with 30 percent, but no new jobs had been created and no less than 25 percent of the adult population between twenty and sixty-five years of age remained outside the regular labor market. The needs were large within health and social care, but those sectors were hopelessly organized.[9] That the Swedish welfare state was characterized by full employment was a myth. Early retirement and sickness absence had become regular features in the Swedish labor market. The construction of the welfare system encouraged this. Sweden was becoming a "soft" state that did not impose any requirements on the citizens and which required the world's highest tax burden to muddle through.[10]

The root of the evil, as Bo saw it, was the law on social services from 1980. In 1994, he launched a frontal attack on it, in an article with the title "Hur kunde det gå så snett?" ("How Could It Get That Wrong?"). He stated that the individual had the right to assistance from the social welfare board for his maintenance and life in general. Bo took this to mean that here was the guarantee that the individual would never have to worry about his maintenance and went on to argue that an ample system of social insurance, early retirement and social service had been built up supported by an administrative bureaucracy and a legal system, by an army of politicians, judges, bureaucrats, and civil servants, whose task it was to make sure that this overloaded system could continue to function for some more time.[11] The system, however, was impossible. Bo argued that "everybody's right to everything" was a mirage, impossible to reach, and which would in addition wipe out the economic and social progress that had been attained.

---

[8] Södersten (2005a).
[9] Södersten (2005b).
[10] Södersten (2005c).
[11] Södersten (1994f).

"Hur kunde det gå så snett?" was not Bo's best article. He almost turned himself inside out and to a large extent his arguments resembled Don Quijote's fight against the windmills. Bo received sharp criticism from the professor of social work in Lund, Ulla Pettersson, who pointed out that the right to social assistance was not unconditional but presupposed that needs could not be satisfied in any other way, meaning that houses, cars, and so on, would have to be sold before a person would qualify. In addition, the creation of the institutions that Bo referred to preceded the law.[12]

Bo, however, persisted in his criticism of the social welfare system. If nothing was done about the structural problems of the welfare state, our welfare would be threatened. At the end of 2000, he again stressed the reluctance to reform.[13] The social insurance system did not work. The state of the economy was what determined the number of people who were away from work. During boom years with plenty of work opportunities, it was easy to stay home. When jobs were scarce, people went to work. The system was sick, stated Bo, but the politicians did nothing to change it. During good years, the social insurance system displayed a considerable deficit. At the time when Bo wrote his article, no more than half of those between sixteen and twenty-four held regular jobs.

Early retirement and sickness absence was not equally distributed across the country. Certain regions, especially the Norrland counties, were conspicuous. In Småland (Gislaved, Gnosjö, Waggeryd, Värnamo), the figures were much lower. There you did not live "on the [local insurance] office (på kassan)." Norrland, on the other hand, was dominated by a "catching culture":

> It begins with picking berries and fishing in the fall and then comes one of the great events of the year, the moose hunt. It continues with small-game hunting and winter fishing and culminates with fishing in the sun during Easter. The planning horizon of the catching culture is short. You don't think of what may come in twenty years' time but are content with a three to four-year planning horizon.[14]

---

[12] Pettersson (1994). Bo's article also invited criticism from four economist colleagues. See Björklund et al. (1994). When a job was available, it had to be accepted.
[13] Södersten (2000c). See also Södersten (2002a).
[14] Södersten (2005d).

CHAPTER 17

Concentration of Power and Corruption

During his years in Parliament, Bo Södersten had gradually become critical of his own party. The reasons were partly personal. He did not make it within the party, a party which he conceived of as too centralized. He developed his argument in an article in *Aktuellt i Politiken*, the Social Democratic weekly.[1] The dictum that all power emanates from the people was a truth with plenty of modification. The parliament was an institution which essentially confirmed decisions which had been made elsewhere, and the individual MPs did not have much of a say. It was not the hand that held the stamp but the stamp. The Swedish Social Democracy was characterized by an extreme concentration of power, to the executive committee and a small group of ministers, and the individual members had to serve as megaphones propagating the party message.

To the extent that they had any influence, this was limited to mainly local and regional questions, questions of concern for the party districts that had elected them. Bo warned that democracy was a frail plant. In order to make it flower, it was necessary to listen to what the common people had to say. The party could not become an ombudsman party governed by a professional party leadership. The basis of the recruitment to the party had to be broadened.

---

[1] Södersten (1988e),

In a talk given a few years later, Bo developed the theme. He described how decisions were made in his own party:

> The Social Democratic group in the parliament meets every Tuesday afternoon when the parliament is in session. A Social Democratic government has to have the support of its own group if it is to get its proposals through Parliament. It is therefore the custom that all proposals are presented to the parliamentary group before they are introduced in the parliament. Usually, the minister in question makes a presentation to the group on Tuesday and the proposal is introduced the following Thursday. It is in the nature of things that it is hardly possible to stage any real discussion ... under such circumstances.[2]

The parliamentary group was large, more than 150 people. Already that made detailed discussions difficult, but it was not part of Social Democratic good manners either to speak too often or to make lengthy statements within the group. The latter was to be regarded as a clearance central, completely subordinate to the party leadership. You couldn't rock the boat. Democracy was the prestige word, but only a democracy controlled by the established politicians. No wonder that the Swedish political parties had lost half of their members in the 1990s.[3]

Bo did not hesitate to call his party "Leninist." When it came to the election of party chairmen, from that of Per Albin and henceforth, there had never been more than a single candidate, and in 1995, it was time again. Ingvar Carlsson wanted Mona Sahlin to succeed him. However, Bo thought that it would be the last time that this could be done. The party had survived itself. Its unique combination of concentration of power and member mobilization would disappear, and it would become a party among other parties.[4] However, Bo was wrong. Sahlin committed the ridiculous mistake of using a government credit card for personal expenses and had to refrain from running. Göran Persson was chosen instead. Mona Sahlin had to wait until 2007—when she was the sole candidate.

Only a few persons were entitled to decide the contents of politics. Bo did not hesitate to charge them. In 1996, he attacked the Prime Minister, Ingvar Carlsson, as responsible for the Swedish crisis.[5] As Minister of

---

[2] Södersten (1993?).
[3] Södersten (2000b).
[4] Södersten (1995e).
[5] Södersten (1996b).

Housing during the 1970s, he had contributed to undermining government finances by exaggerated subsidization of construction. In 1996, he wanted to increase taxes for high-income earners, which Bo argued would reduce the efficiency of the Swedish economy and undermine the recent tax reform. He was a weak party leader who wanted to please the Left in order to remain in power.

The political centralization within the Social Democratic party went hand in hand with the increasing symbiosis between the party and the trade union movement. The person to be blamed for this was Olof Palme, who had not been able to keep the vested interest represented by the LO at bay and had not managed to maintain the balance between the private and the public sector.[6] Palme and his generation were the prisoners of collectivistic thought.[7] The earlier compromises in labor market matters were gone and the trade unions had resorted to legislation to make sure that their demands were met. Palme could not resist but accepted to run union errands in exchange for votes. Vote buying and clientelism characterized the relation between the party and the unions.[8]

The Swedish Social Democracy was weak. The party was plagued by a systematic incompetence cult. It was intellectually and morally bankrupt, and it looked backward instead of forward.[9] The recruitment to the party left a lot to be desired. The Social Democratic group in Parliament had long been weak and new members were recruited in a way which bred incompetence, one of two below forty and one of two a woman, instead of using the self-evident democratic principle: free elections. It was nothing but a farce. Ignorant and unexperienced politicians did not rock the boat but followed the unwritten laws of the party, above all that of complete loyalty.

The Limits of Democracy

The centralization and the cult of silence led to the question of how democracy was faring in Sweden. Bo did not think it worked particularly well.[10] For a political regime to be considered democratic, four require-

---

[6] Södersten (1996c).
[7] See also Södersten (1997f).
[8] See also Södersten (1998b).
[9] Södersten (1996e).
[10] Södersten (1997g).

ments had to be met: free elections, changes of power, constitutional freedoms and rights, and efficient exercise of power. Bo argued that Sweden was deficient with respect to the second and fourth criteria. The power hegemony of the Social Democrats had never really been challenged, in spite of the fact that other parties had been in government for a few periods.

The Social Democrats remained in power after the 2002 elections. This was not good since it cemented the impression that Sweden was, if not a one-party state, a one-party regime,[11] something that would guarantee that nothing changed. The hegemony also influenced how power was wielded. It was difficult to oppose the party. The public administration was dominated by the Social Democrats, and those who wanted to make a career, that is, those with ambitions, virtually always ended up on the side of those in power, not least on the local and county level.[12]

Bo argued that all political exercise of power had to be tamed, limited, and controlled so that it did not degenerate into oppression. At the same time, power had to be exercised in a competent and efficient way. As Bo saw it, this was the case only with monetary policy, an area handled by the Riksbank and not by the parliament, by competent specialists. The same kind of solution could be implemented in a number of other areas: tax policy, health care, housing policy, energy policy, and transport policy. Maybe the time had come for a thorough overhaul of the Swedish democracy.

As could be expected, Bo was criticized from all quarters. Democracy was in danger and had to be defended at any cost. Bo was a totalitarian and a representative of shady interests who called the entire system of parliamentary democracy into question. It was impossible to leave decisions with respect to the political *goals* to experts. That kind of decisions were collective and had to be made by the parliament. Technocracy and bureaucracy would easily breed corruption, especially if they were allowed to build their own, closed, worlds.[13]

The Västerås bishop, Claes-Bertil Ytterberg, even compared Bo's ideas to those of Adolf Hitler.[14] And then, an entire university department, that of journalism, media, and communication, at Stockholm University,

---

[11] Södersten (2002c).
[12] Södersten (1997g).
[13] Bergström (1997).
[14] Ytterberg (1997).

jumped on him. Bo's recipe would lead to despotism. The arrogance of power would rule in his imaginary society. Bo did not even pretend that he adhered to the principles of democracy.[15]

CORRUPT POLITICIANS

In a 1995 article, Bo took his argument about politics one step further. He accused the politicians of corruption.[16] Again his point of departure was the swollen public sector and the mistaken prioritization within it. It was OK to switch between the Labour Market Board programs for unemployed and unemployment benefits as long as you were "at the disposal of the labor market." It was enough for a person to have had a paid job for seventy-five days to live on benefits and unemployment programs for the rest of his life.

Bo asked why Sweden had ended up in a situation where the senseless public expenditures skyrocketed, and the tax burden was all too high. His answer was phrased in moral terms, in terms of corruption. He defined two types of corruption: the one where you were after personal gains and the one where you try to conquer power by buying votes and distributing advantages. The former was absent from Swedish politics but not the latter. This was what had produced the overdimensioned public sector, the monstrous tax burden, and the public debt swamp.

---

[15] Fornäs et al. (1998).
[16] Södersten (1995a). The article was translated into French (Södersten 1995b).

CHAPTER 18

Systemic Defects

After leaving Parliament in 1988, Bo began to argue that the Swedish economy was plagued by severe systemic defects. Sweden was a country with huge problems and little faith in the future.

It was sliding downward in international comparison. The high marginal tax rates discouraged people from working and making money. The economic systemic defects, like the low productivity of the public sector were well-known, but not the political ones. The Social Democratic party was governed far too much from the top. Sweden had become a society where ownership of houses and shares mattered more than the ability to work. The concentration of power within the Social Democratic party had led to a populist policy.[1]

Bo identified those responsible for the systemic defects: the Social Democratic leaders, notably the high priests: Olof Palme and Ingvar Carlsson.[2] The efficiency that the Social Democratic power apparatus had displayed from the beginning of the 1930s to the end of the 1960s had been replaced by populism: symbolic issues and hope for a fast answer from the voters. The party was characterized by reserve and discipline. The leaders seldom had problems getting acceptance for their views and a good ear made for a place at the flesh pots.

[1] Södersten (1989d).
[2] Södersten (1989e).

The Social Democrats were led by the nose by the trade unions.[3] The 1980s had been a decade of wage increases completely incompatible with the development of the economy. The Social Democrats refused to face the truth. The trade unions could demand anything and get away with it. Given the 1990 tax reform, curbing wage demands ought not to be a problem, but then Ingvar Carlsson had to show some real leadership with respect to economic policy.

Time after time, Bo pointed to the systemic errors in childcare, housing, and health care.[4] He had little hope that things would change since the Social Democrats were an internally divided party that lacked a firm leadership intent on reforms. Bo wanted a perestroika within the party.

The Social Democrats had been able to set the political agenda for sixty years, but instead of using market-related incentives, it had resorted to a requisition mentality where the burden of the expansion of the public sector was put on the taxpayers.[5] Unless something was done to change this, the Social Democrats risked being reduced to a party of discontent on the left without relevance for the future Swedish development [6]

Low-Productive Health Care

The worst systemic defect of all was the degeneration of the welfare state. Bo exemplified by using the health care sector. One of his debate articles was given the provocative title "Kvinnor har för höga löner" ("Female Wages Are Too High") (as it seems by the debate page editor).[7] In this article, Bo compared the development of productivity and wages in the "male" industrial sector and the "female" public sector. The wage increases for industrial workers were lower than the productivity increases. The difference was taxed away by the state through the payroll tax. In the public sector, the situation was completely different. The productivity had declined for a long time and in order to keep production up, resources had to be added continuously. Nurses and auxiliaries were subsidized by the industrial workers. The marginal productivity of these groups did not differ significantly from zero. One of the major hospitals in the country had

[3] Södersten (1990h).
[4] Södersten (1990i).
[5] Södersten (1991b).
[6] Södersten (1991c).
[7] Södersten (1995c).

300 redundant employees. It was obvious that structural reforms were needed. Wages had to match productivity. The principle of equal pay for all work was unsound. The blame for this situation Bo put on the Swedish Metal Workers Union which had not been able to defend the interests of its members.[8]

In Bo's world there was no place for child and health care personnel who regularly stayed away from work. Productivity was low in health care. Of the 85,000 employees in the Stockholm region, every day of the year, 27,000 never showed up: an absurd situation.[9] It was not only among nurses and auxiliaries that you could make efficiency gains. In 1996, Bo and his nephew, the physician Anders Milton, the managing director of the Swedish Medical Association, published an article that contended that Sweden had too many physicians. The number of physicians had trebled since 1970 but the number of doctor appointments was only half of the Western European average. However, the politicians were not particularly interested in increasing efficiency.[10]

The problems of the public sector were also exposed in the geriatric care.[11] This was managed by the municipalities which were free to determine the charges. Bo contended that many of them had lost their sense of proportions and had converted themselves into robber institutions which confiscated the incomes and wealth of the elderly. The municipalities lacked the ability to save and often had large budget deficits. The financing of the geriatric care had to be reformed and some kind of insurance system should be created.

In 1996, Bo suggested a way to increase female wages—a way which was related to their productivity.[12] His recipe consisted in a transfer of activities from the public to the private sector. It was simply a sexist myth that women could only work in the public sector. Privatization would lead to competition, safe jobs for women, and market-determined wages. Production would become efficient, and only the firms that met the expectations of the market, the preferences of the consumers, would survive.

That the welfare state could be reformed was proved by the Dutch experience. In the same way as Sweden, Holland had had an

---

[8] Södersten (1998c). Bo's provocation met heavy criticism. See e. g. Hedwall (1995), Janson (1995) and Nordh and Pettersson (1995).
[9] Södersten (1992e).
[10] Milton and Södersten (1996).
[11] Södersten (1998a).
[12] Södersten (1996d).

overdimensioned public sector. However, the Dutch had pulled themselves together and reduced the public spending. The wage increases were held back through voluntary agreements between employers and employees. Employment increased and it even proved possible to get many people who had chosen early retirement back into the labor market. The Dutch success was due to coalition governments between center-right parties and Social Democrats. This provided a model for Sweden to follow.[13]

Bo Södersten's appreciation of the market mechanism underwent a drastic change over time. When Assar Lindbeck in 1972 praised the qualities of the market, he immediately attacked him. Bo thought that it was no use discussing how the Swedish industrial sector should be financed by the banks unless you discussed the need for technical change in the industrial sector at the same time. This called for concentrated, planned action and finance via public funds. Bo's and Lindbeck's visions of the decentralized society differed radically.[14]

In the late 1990s, Bo's views of the market mechanism had changed completely. The stagnation of the Swedish economy was a result of the Social Democratic reluctance to accept the market economy. Sweden had a structural problem: high taxes, high public expenditures and a non-functioning labor market, but the Social Democrats refused to realize this. They were stuck with an old-fashioned Keynesian philosophy which did not solve the problem. Increased public expenditures would simply lead to inflation. The market economy had to be extended to the public sector, providing signals of how resources should be allocated, of what should expand and what should contract.[15]

REFORMING THE WELFARE STATE

When Bo Södersten came to the Jönköping International Business School in 1998, he initiated a project called "Globalization and the Welfare State." This resulted, among other things, in two books that he edited himself, *Globalization and the Welfare State*[16] and *Den problematiska tryggheten – välfärdsstaten under tre decennier* (*The Problematic Security – the Welfare State During Three Decades*).[17] In an article in *Dagens Nyheter* in

---
[13] Södersten (1998f).
[14] Södersten (1972).
[15] Södersten (1997e).
[16] Södersten (2004a).
[17] Södersten (2006a).

2002, he reported some of the most important findings.[18] Sweden had an open unemployment rate of 4 percent, but if instead you calculated how many people that did not work, you arrived at much higher figures. No less than 23 percent of the population of working age did not work. If you wanted a correct idea of the situation in the Swedish labor market, it was not enough to count the openly unemployed and those in vocational training courses. You had to add those on the long-term sick list, those in early retirement, those studying (often because they did not get any job) and those who had left the labor market for other reasons, and that left all those who had reported sick and did not go to work, but who formally belonged to the "working" category.

The Swedish model did not work anymore. Sweden was no longer a welfare state. Germany, Great Britain, Denmark, and Holland had realized that the time had come for a reform. The health insurance system sent the wrong kind of signals. It was obvious that the norms related to work and use of the privileges of the welfare state had changed. The social insurance system had to change too.

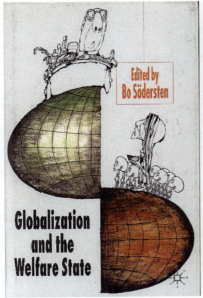

Reforming the welfare state

[18] Södersten (2002b).

In his own chapter in *Globalization and the Welfare State*, Bo describes the welfare society as a general equilibrium system, a system where changes in the private sector, the public sector, and the welfare system affect each other.[19] The reduced growth since the beginning of the 1970s had increased the rate of unemployment, and the generous construction of the social welfare system had reduced the willingness to work.

In the second book from the welfare state project, the point of departure was the early 1970s, the period when Sweden began its journey from high to low growth, and the expansion of the welfare state thereafter. The purpose of the book was not to begin a polemic or to discuss the pros and contras of the welfare state. It simply intended to sketch some of the major problems —the ones likely to be on the future agenda.

Bo's chapter—the longest in the book—is an extended version of the chapter in the English volume, a somewhat curious mixture of the Swedish economic development 1970–2000 and his own experience in Parliament.[20] During the 1970s, a decade of low economic growth, Sweden got the highest tax burden among the OECD countries. This reduced the willingness to work and the employment in the private sector. The 1980s were a decade of expansion of the public sector and of wages determined by the demands of those working in the low-productivity sectors. Little was done to prevent the overheating of the economy. The problems continued during the first half of the 1990s, when half a million jobs were lost. During this decade, growth again was based on the export sector. Flexible exchange rates were introduced, and Sweden entered the EU. Still, growth was jobless. The Swedish welfare policy contributed to this by creating negative attitudes to work. Bo wondered whether the traditionally strong Swedish work ethic was being dissolved due to high marginal tax rate and generous social insurance benefits.

---

[19] Södersten (2004b).
[20] Södersten (2006b).

CHAPTER 19

Book Reviews and Biography

One of Bo Södersten's best genres was book reviews. He had an ability to find interesting works, and most of the time he treated them in a personal way. Bo was interested in history and the interpretation of it. The fact that he was critical of collectivism made him read the Keynes biographer Robert Skidelsky's *The World after Communism* which he contrasted with the Marxist historian Eric Hobsbawm's *Age of Extremes: The Short Twentieth Century 1914–1991*.[1] Skidelsky demonstrated how collectivism in various ways put a stamp on most of the twentieth century through the Keynesian ideas, the expansion of the public sector, and the increasing enthusiasm for economic planning. Hobsbawm, in turn, had a wide perspective and an overview. None of them, however, had the analytical economic apparatus required to explain the events that led to the fall of Communism in Eastern Europe.

In 1996, the Uppsala economic historian Lars Magnusson published his *Sveriges ekonomiska historia* (*An Economic History of Sweden*).[2] Bo did not think that he managed to bring out the most important period, the one he had kept hammering himself: the age of high growth, 1870–1970. Magnusson was influenced by the *Annales* school stress of mentalities, but

[1] Skidelsky (1995), Hobsbawm (1994), Södersten (1996f).
[2] Magnusson (1996), English translation: Magnusson (2007).

Bo contended that he had missed the development of the Swedish mentality during the hundred glorious years.[3]

Biographies

Another, literary, genre that appealed to Bo was biography. He reviewed Olof Ehrenkrona's 1991 biography of Curt Nicolin, the managing director and chairman of the board of ASEA and the man who reconstructed the SAS.[4] Bo thought that it was too much of a hagiography, but credited Ehrenkrona for using an analytical approach and portraying his subject against the background of the general economic and social development in Sweden.[5]

That Bo would be drawn to politicians' memoirs does not surprise anyone. In 1991, Kjell-Olof Feldt published *Alla dessa dagar* (*All These Days*), about his years in the government, 1982–1990.[6] Bo jumped it.[7] The book was well-written with a knowledgeable political analysis. The question was rather whether it could justify Feldt's contributions as Minister of Finance. Had his economic policy benefited the country?

Later the same year, another former Social Democratic minister—Anna-Greta Leijon, ex Assistant Minister of Labor and Minister of Justice—joined Feldt.[8] Bo both praised and criticized her. She was open and did not hesitate to display her weak side, and she was a warm, gifted and courageous politician who managed to handle the bombing of the West German embassy in Stockholm in 1975 and the attempt by a German terrorist group to kidnap her two years later. However, she was not a good Minister of Labor and fortunately she did not succeed Feldt as Minister of Finance. She lacked the necessary qualifications for that.[9]

Two years after Feldt and Leijon, the former Minister of Social Affairs and, later Minister for Foreign Affairs, Sten Andersson, published his recollections.[10] He was definitely not a politician that Bo liked, especially not after their clash over the devaluation compensation to the pensioners in

---
[3] Södersten (1997b).
[4] Ehrenkrona (1991).
[5] Södersten (1991e).
[6] Feldt (1991).
[7] Södersten (1991f).
[8] Leijon (1991).
[9] Södersten (1991k).
[10] Andersson (1993).

1984. Bo somewhat reluctantly had to admit Feldt's merits, and he could stand Leijon. Andersson was a very different politician who had written a book that aimed at protecting the party and which in addition displayed an anecdotic attitude to life. He hid his unique position in politics, first as secretary of the Social Democratic party and then as minister and member of the inner circle. His warmth was directed only toward the party members, never toward outsiders, and he was a completely irresponsible minister. The compensation to the pensioners made it impossible to put the economy on a sound basis and contributed heavily to the economic crisis of the 1990s.[11]

Bo liked Annika Åhnberg's memoirs, from 1999, a great deal better.[12] She was a bit of an unlikely person for Bo to write about. Åhnberg had entered Parliament in 1988 for the Left Party—the Communists and Bo did not like Communists. However, she reacted against Communism when the Berlin wall fell and thereafter joined the Social Democrats. Surprisingly, she became Minister of Agriculture in 1996, she realized the need for reform of the agricultural policy, and she dared to speak out.[13]

One of the heavyweights of the Swedish Social Democracy during the twentieth century was Gunnar Sträng, Minister of Finance. In 1992, the first volume of the economic historian Anders L. Johansson's biography of him appeared.[14] Sträng was a person that mattered to Bo, who obviously enjoyed Johansson's book but thought that it was a bit too flattering and lacked the wide perspective that would have provided a background to Sträng's life.[15]

In his book reviews, Bo of course also paid attention to the great economists. He thought that Richard Swedberg's 1991 biography of Joseph Schumpeter[16] was sensationally good and extremely coherent.[17] In his review, Bo highlighted the antagonism between Schumpeter and Keynes and stressed the solid anchorage of the former in real-world problems, a detail to be noted in a time when economic analysis tended to distance itself from them.

---

[11] Södersten (1993e).
[12] Åhnberg (1999).
[13] Södersten (1999f).
[14] Johansson (1992).
[15] Södersten (1993b).
[16] Swedberg (1991).
[17] Södersten (1992f).

In 1998, a "double autobiography" was published, the one by Milton Friedman and his wife, Rose.[18] Bo reviewed it, mainly as an excuse to present his own views of Milton.[19] It was not true that he was Pinochet's economic advisor, and he had not trained the latter's economists, *Los Chicago Boys*. He had only been in Chile once and there was an old agreement between Chicago and Chilean universities about PhD studies in Chicago. Bo stressed his role as advisor to Nixon and Reagan and his very active participation in the public debate. Friedman was the answer of the right to Keynes.

Nobel Laureates

A different kind on "review" was the comparison that Bo made between the scientific contributions of Bertil Ohlin and Gunnar Myrdal in 1999.[20] In spite of all their common characteristics, according to Bo, there was a fundamental difference between the two. There was not a single theoretical achievement connected with Myrdal's name. That he had received the Sveriges Riksbank Prize in Economic Sciences in Memory of Alfred Nobel amounted to pure provincialism. He was obsolete. The case of Ohlin was different. The Heckscher-Ohlin and factor price equalization theorems were here to stay. Ohlin's approach was still vigorous and had inspired many later economists.

The prize in economics was a matter of concern for Bo. In 2001, he looked back on the years that had passed since it was awarded for the first time, in 1969.[21] In spite of the fact that Myrdal had received it, that Friedman had been met by political demonstrations and that Joan Robinson had been sidestepped, the process had worked decently well in the 1970s and 1980s. There were plenty of capable people to reward, people with strong roots in the social sciences. Thereafter, however, inspired by the natural sciences, theorems, and econometric and mathematical methods had been favored, and the links to the social sciences had been weakened. Bo was worried that this trend would continue and that hence the prize would lose its interest.

---

[18] Friedman and Friedman (1998).
[19] Södersten (1998d).
[20] Södersten (1999e).
[21] Södersten (2001d).

Culture

Bo did not let go of the cultural themes either. He portrayed his friend the cartoonist—one of the greatest in the political genre ever—EWK (Ewert Karlsson) with whom had visited Africa and Latin America and practiced fly-fishing, offering some snapshots from their trips.[22] In 2000, he praised the authorship of Björn Larsson, professor of French in Lund, [23] who at the time had published one book of short stories and four novels,[24] and who in 1998 had received the prestigious French *Prix Médicis étranger* for *Le capitaine et les rêves*, the translation of his third novel in Swedish.[25] Bo was angry because these books had hardly received any attention at all from the Swedish cultural establishment.

Torsten Gårdlund

In 2003, Torsten Gårdlund, Bo's predecessor as professor of international economics in Lund, passed away. Lars Jonung, Bo, and I wrote an obituary. Somewhat later, Bo called and asked me whether I wanted to collaborate with him on an article about Gårdlund for the series of portraits of economists regularly featured by *Ekonomisk Debatt*. I accepted, and we began to write. In the end we produced two different versions of the article, a biographical book and an introductory essay on Gårdlund the essayist for a posthumously published book of essays of his that we edited.[26]

The writing process was not easy, for Bo's health had begun to deteriorate. A few years later, he would be officially diagnosed with Alzheimer's disease, but his illness had begun to make itself noticed already around this time. This made it difficult for him to concentrate and above all to write, so we developed a method whereby I read Gårdlund's works and we discussed them together before our thoughts were put on paper.

At any rate, we painted a few different-size portraits of Gårdlund. He was a very productive economist, with twenty published books during his lifetime. Torsten Gårdlund had his education from the Stockholm School of Economics where he graduated at the end of 1932. Thereafter, he

---

[22] Södersten (2003b).
[23] Södersten (2000/2001).
[24] Larsson (1980, 1992, 1995, 1997, 1999a).
[25] Larsson (1999b).
[26] Lundahl and Södersten (2004, 2009b), English translations: Lundahl and Södersten (2015), Lundahl and Södersten (2009a, 2010).

chose an academic career, but at the time he could not pursue PhD studies at the SSE, so Gårdlund moved to Stockholm College, where he first got a licentiate degree on a book on economics and social policy in France between 1918 and 1938,[27] and in 1942 defended his doctoral dissertation on the Swedish industrialization process, *Industrialismens samhälle* (*Industrial Society*).[28]

In 1947, Torsten Gårdlund became professor of economics at the Stockholm School of Economics, where he remained until 1963. During his time there, he published collections of essays and wrote monographs about Swedish companies and industrial finance and, above all, his masterly biography of Knut Wicksell: *Knut Wicksell. Rebell i det nya riket*, translated as *The Life of Knut Wicksell*.[29] After spending some time in Morocco and Tunisia as an economic advisor, Gårdlund, in 1965, moved to Lund, to a newly created chair in international economics. His years there were productive, with three books on economic development issues,[30] an impressive biography of the banker Marcus Wallenberg, Sr., one of the most important figures in the Swedish industrial development during the interwar years,[31] followed by more biographic works and company monographs.

Bo and I labeled Torsten Gårdlund Sweden's only "literary" economist. No one came close to him when it came to constructing elegant phrases, which he often thought out during his morning rides. (Gårdlund bred Anglo-Arab horses on his stud farm outside Lund.) He demonstrated this skill in all his works, but mainly in his biographies and essays. The latter was a genre especially favored by him. He had an unusual ability to find unexpected and intriguing themes which he developed in cultural articles in *Svenska Dagbladet* and later republished in his collections of essays.

---

[27] Gårdlund (1939).
[28] Gårdlund (1942).
[29] Gårdlund (1956) and (1958), respectively.
[30] Gårdlund (1965, 1967, 1968).
[31] Gårdlund (1976).

TORSTEN GÅRDLUND
Det goda livets ekonom

MATS LUNDAHL & BO SÖDERSTEN

TIMBRO

Relaxing is part of the good life

Gårdlund also had a well-developed philosophy about how to write biography, a philosophy which he had developed himself, since, as he claimed, he could not find any works to guide him when he took his first steps in this genre. He aimed for the soft flow of the good novel, cultivating a style that never turned extravagant. The text should flow gently and against this background you could permit yourself occasional bursts of linguistic lightning.

Torsten Gårdlund was a man who enjoyed the good life. One of his most memorable essays has precisely this title. It dealt with the kind of society which was found in the writings of the utopian Socialists: a society which they had endowed with everything that they had been forced to forsake in their own lifetime. It is impossible to escape from the feeling that Torsten Gårdlund shared most of their preferences.

CHAPTER 20

Who Was He, Really?

All who knew Bo Södersten realized that he was an extremely complex person.[1] He could be utterly charming, but he could also turn people off with brusque manners in situations where you would not have expected it. He was inherently contradictory, not always rational, and could quickly swing from one extreme to the other. Bo's personality resembled a jigsaw puzzle with very many pieces—pieces which did always fit into each other.

Most of the time, Bo was in a mood which spread good vibrations in the room, irradiating pleasure and the joy of life. He could be jovial and talk about things that he liked in a way that enthralled and inspired his listeners, both small talk and incisive comments on social issues: minor impromptu lectures. But he could also become a pain in the neck in situations where he was tired, under pressure, had found an issue which irritated him, or was dissatisfied with life in general.

---

[1] The present chapter presents my personal view of Bo Södersten. I have had the privilege of receiving personal recollections of him by Mats Bergstrand, Yves Bourdet, Henrik Braconier, Karolina Ekholm, Gunnar Eriksson, Kjell-Olof Feldt, Helena Frielingsdorf Lundqvist, Per-Axel Frielingsdorf, Birgit Friggebo, Anders Milton, Inga Persson, Jeanie and Lennart Petersson, Lars Pettersson, Lars Ramqvist, Ann-Marie and Bo Sandelin, Fredrik Sjöholm, Anna, Astrid and Wiktor Södersten. They have all influenced my presentation, refuting or confirming some of my preconceived notions, but it should be stressed that my ambition has been to provide my own subjective picture of a man that I liked and interacted with a lot.

© The Author(s), under exclusive license to Springer Nature Switzerland AG 2022
M. Lundahl, *Bo Södersten from Left to Right*, Palgrave Studies in the History of Economic Thought,
https://doi.org/10.1007/978-3-031-09101-8_20

Bo was a pronounced egocentric. He loved to speak about himself, also in situations where the topic was unrelated to his person. He disliked being criticized, especially in front of other people. Then he usually became arrogant and did his best to crush the critic completely. He displayed a complete absence of self-criticism and avoided situations where he had to admit that he was not right and situations which called for a solution but which he was not sure that he could handle. His egocentricity, however, also formed part of his charm. He was an expert on dropping one-liners about his own person, like on one occasion when he had received the first copy of his latest book: "You are struck by the high quality." Comments like that could make an entire room crack up.

Family Life

Bo's family life was complicated. He met his first wife, Astrid (née Wallin) during his study years in Uppsala. Astrid was born in Jakobstad in Österbotten in Finland in 1934, where her father had founded and run one of the most modern dairies in the country until he was drafted into military service during the Winter War and was wounded twice. The family left Finland in 1941, before the Continuation War broke out, and ended up buying the Årsta farm outside Uppsala. After her graduation from high school, Astrid studied French, English, and pedagogy at Uppsala University, where she met Bo in 1957, and they quickly became a couple. Bo and Astrid married in Copenhagen in the fall of 1960. Astrid worked as a teacher of French and English and helped supporting the family while Bo was finishing his PhD.

Bo had four children with Astrid: Anna, born in 1961; Henrik, 1962; Erika, 1968; and Wiktor, 1972. Their relation was a stormy one. Both were short-tempered and easily got into heated arguments, but they were also genuinely devoted to each other, so for many years they managed to patch up their marriage, and they kept their feelings for each other also after their divorce. Their family life was complicated by the fact that the family moved around a lot: from Stockholm to the United States and back to Sweden, thereafter back to the United States again for some years and from there to Lund. There the children had some un-interrupted schooling time between 1967 and 1975, until again it was time for the United States, and then to move to Gothenburg and finally back to Lund once more. In addition, Bo went on a number of trips to developing countries for work reasons: Swaziland and Botswana, Cuba and Chile. He was frequently absent and was not present at the birth of some of his children.

Bo could be very sweet and considerate toward his children, and his intelligence and erudition was a source of inspiration for them. But he was not the kind of father who would easily crawl on the floor to play with children, and he could also be very demanding, especially when it came to their school notes, subjecting them to long interrogations about their latest exam.

In 1973, Bo began a relationship with Helga Frielingsdorf. They had two children: Helena, 1976, and Per-Axel, 1983. The relationship lasted for more than two decades. It worked because few demands were put on him. Bo visited Helga and the children regularly, about every second month, and he went on vacation with them for a week or more every year, until Helga ended the relationship in 1997. At that point, Bo decided not to see the children anymore and abruptly cut off the contact.

Bo and Astrid divorced in 1983. Thereafter, Bo lived with Gun Östlund, a former neighbor in Lund, for a few years, before he met Birgit Friggebo in Parliament in 1988. Birgit's family comes from Friggeråker in Falköping in western Sweden (hence her last name). She is one of the most well-known Liberal politicians in the country. Birgit was an MP for the Liberal Party between 1979 and 1982 and 1985 to 1997, Minister of Housing between 1976 and 1982 and Minister of Culture (as well as Immigration and Gender Equality) from 1991 to 1994. After retiring from Parliament, she was the governor of the county of Jönköping between 1998 and 2003. She will always be inexorably connected with, and remembered by, the Swedish people for the so-called friggebod (bod = shed). She initiated the legislation which made it possible to build a house of up to 10 square meters (subsequently increased to 15 square meters) without having to apply for a construction permit, a measure which became enormously popular.[2]

Bo and Birgit married in 1997. Their marriage was stable, in spite of the fact that their political backgrounds differed substantially. They met relatively late in life, and they had no children in common. Birgit appreciated the fact that Bo was an intellectual, and they traveled a lot together. Bo, in turn, was able to profit from Birgit's position as County Governor

---

[2] For her own account, see Friggebo (2011).

and former minister, and the contact opportunities which this offered. He was far from immune to invitations to royal dinners, Nobel dinners, and similar occasions.

Mission Social Climbing accomplished. Left to right: Queen Silvia, Bo, Birgit. (Courtesy Birgit Friggebo)

Bo also established an extremely good relation with the local Jönköping elite, notably with Stig Fredriksson and his wife Christina Hamrin. The Hamrin family had owned Herenco, a company active in manufacturing, printing, and media for three generations. In addition to being the managing director of Herenco, Fredriksson was the editor-in-chief of *Jönköpings-Posten* (owned by Herenco) where Bo became a frequent contributor of articles.[3] He also received research grants from the Hamrin Foundation.

Living with Bo was anything but easy. He had a solid reputation for being a ladies' man. In his characteristic, his admirer Hans O. Sjöström sums him up: "... he was a sharp and clear-minded debater and wrote better than most people. The fact that in addition he was considered to be keen on chicks did not reduce our admiration for him."[4] In his draft

---

[3] See Gustafsson (2017) for the story of Stig Fredriksson and the newspaper.
[4] Sjöström (1987), p. 84. See also Kokk (n.d.).

memoirs Bo himself writes about his Uppsala says: "... in any case, for me, there were lots of girls, or rather, women," a fact that he was obviously proud of: "more about that later."[5] (He never got around to that in his draft.) Bo was "always on the hunt,"[6] maintaining extramarital amorous relations, and he loved to brag about them. He "knew his thing," but the thing easily backfired. On one occasion he was sued for breach of promise to contract matrimony by a girl who had divorced in order to marry him and had to pay.

Student Relations

Being a ladies' man did not make life easier for Bo, but he somehow managed to keep his family life together over the years and he shared it willingly. Those of us who were his students were invited to his home with our own families, which led to a stable social network which met regularly for dinners together with him and other faculty members. This was invaluable. We were socialized little by little into the academic community until we became full-fledged members of it.

This does not mean that it was easy to be Bo's student. The undergraduate seminars in international economics all too often began with a scolding of the opponent on the paper that was to be discussed. The opponent was incapable of asking a single intelligent question. Then, Bo took over the opposition himself and proceeded to deliver a harsh critique, frequently ridiculing the victim in the process. Not everybody was able to handle that in a situation where you knew that he would be the one deciding the mark on your paper.

Bo was not mean, but he could be very blunt. He was very intelligent, appreciated people who were smart and well-read and did not tolerate fools who were unable to come up with analytical arguments. But Bo also needed resistance. The worst thing you could do was to bend over and let him have it his way. If you persisted and argued your case, you stood a better chance, unless he had a bad day and chose to mock what you had written. It was easy to get into an argument with him. When I defended my own undergraduate paper, we disagreed violently on one issue, almost to the point where we both stood up. However, the matter was settled after the seminar. I would write a paper and straighten out the issue. Then,

[5] Södersten (2001a).
[6] Milton (2011), p. 23.

we proceeded to have dinner together in the best restaurant in Lund. Bo was hot-tempered but he easily forgave. But you had to learn. If you wanted to hang out with him, there were certain things that you had to accept in order to get to the better part of him. You simply had to shrug your shoulders, not pay attention to everything he said, and try to change the topic of the conversation.

 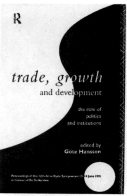 

The three festschrifts

Those who Bo liked, he supported 100 percent. If he believed in you, you knew that he was behind you, come rain or come shine, should you need his support, and he went out of his way in critical situations to ensure that things worked out the way they should. He took all opportunities to point out the excellence of his students to the people he met. He saw to it that they got project and travel money, he persuaded publishers to accept their manuscripts, and he got them consultancy jobs. It was no coincidence that he was given three festschrifts: one at his fiftieth birthday, one at his sixtieth, and one at his eightieth.[7]

Bo was a good lecturer who inspired the students by his enthusiasm. He always contended that pedagogy was a non-issue in the university setting. If you knew your subject, you just went into the classroom and explained it. That was precisely what he did. He was not an active supervisor in the sense that he provided topics that the students could write about. Nor did he make detailed comments. He was more concerned with the overall

[7] Lundahl (1981), Hansson (1993), Lundahl (2011).

structure and presentation. The seminars were the most important part of his supervisory activities. They worked well in Lund, both before and after his time in Parliament. In Gothenburg, which was a bit of a run-down department when Bo got his chair there, he saw to it that the students would have to present thesis drafts regularly. In Jönköping he made the Friday seminars the hub of the activities of the economics department.

Bo and his crew, 1972. Back row, left to right: Henrik Södersten, Inga Persson, Hanna Lundahl, Maja Lundahl, Anna Södersten, Ann-Marie Sandelin, Magnus Sandelin, Bo Sandelin, Mats Lundahl. Front row, left to right: Maria Sandelin, Astrid Södersten, Bo Södersten, Erika Södersten

The seminars to a large extent were run by the students themselves. We served as opponents on each other's drafts. Bo made sure that an opponent was appointed to deliver the main criticism in each seminar. It was not always that he had read the chapter that was discussed very carefully himself, but he sometimes resorted to following the general drift of the discussion and add comments of his own. We had to come up with our own suggestions for thesis topics, and he never questioned them. He managed to make his students feel that they had accomplished something. The seminars also served to create social cohesion in the group, a cohesion which was further reinforced by Bo's generous invitations to his home. He made his students feel that they were a unique group around him.

The Academic

Simplifying a bit, Bo Södersten's professional career may be divided into three phases: that of the academic, that of the MP, and that of the debater. The first phase covered his study years in Uppsala and Stockholm and his years as a researcher and teacher. In one sense it lasted all the way until his retirement, but Bo Södersten, the academic, was active mainly until he was elected to Parliament, in 1979. He remained there until 1988, and then of course it was parliamentary work, plus the writing of debate articles that dominated. The third phase, which began when he left Parliament in 1988, was dominated by a frenetically impatient production of newspaper articles about all kinds of subjects. He had written articles for many years, but with the exception of the year with *Aftonbladet*, 1971–1972, not as intensely as he would do when he had formally left politics.

Bo's academic production is not very large. It is limited to the unpublished licentiate thesis, his doctoral dissertation, the book on housing, some articles and chapters in scientific books, and the Gårdlund biography. To this you have to add his contributions to the textbook genre, mainly *International Economics*, which was the first modern textbook in international economics, the macro book, the anthologies about the Swedish economy that he edited and the ones on development economics that he and I edited together. However, his textbook production to a large extent amounts to "writing for money." *International Economics* was a commercial success and of course stimulated Bo to seek other lucrative markets.

The only times that Bo penetrated the world of theoretical economics dominated by models was when he wrote his dissertation and the articles that followed it. It is evident that he was not quite comfortable with modeling. He had studied humanities in high school—Latin and Greek—so his mathematical schooling was limited. He had to learn, course by course, and in the end on his own, when he was about to write his dissertation. Mathematics was not his bag, and his critics were quick to point out that he had problems interpreting his algebra. It was instead the application of economic theory that was Bo's forte. He had a knack for converting what he had learned from theoretical articles into practical economic policy, and he frequently made reference to economic theory in his more popular writings.

Bo did not quite have the stamina required for continued academic writings. Once you have received your chair, you don't have to produce anymore. The informal Swedish history of economic doctrines is full of examples. Bo obtained his professorship at a time when the trick was to just clear the bar. It did not matter if it quivered. Then you could retire and enjoy your otium. Bo was, however, not lazy in any way. On the contrary. Lying on the sofa did not appeal to him, but he preferred to direct his energy toward issues outside academia.

As is well known, the picture of the academic/genius is a false one. Of course, you don't make a career without inspiration and ideas, but the inspiration does not have to be divine. You can make it anyway, but seldom without a large measure of transpiration. In the end, this leads to some kind of publication but not to sensational publicity, and Bo did not in any way despise publicity. On the contrary, he actively sought it through his articles in the daily newspapers.

Bo's best genre was the political and economic essay, mainly in the somewhat longer format. His pieces from the late 1950s and the 1960s can still be read with pleasure, since they represent a forceful and attractive combination of erudition, ideologically based reflection and stylistic ability. His advocacy of the labor-managed economy is also still worth a mass even though the idea fell flat. There you meet a man trying to steer a course between the two extremes of centralized Socialism and private market capitalism, attempting to create an economy based on solidarity and humanism.

Political Failure

Bo came from a working-class family. He was the only one in the family who had been given an opportunity to study. This was probably what accounted for his ambitions. The family ethic was strict. You had to do a good job, whatever you were doing, but you should also demand your rights. When I first met Bo in 1968, he was 100 percent intent on becoming professor. Once this had been achieved, he gave vent to his political ambitions, inherited from home. He made sure that he made it into Parliament, and once he had been elected, his next aim was to become a minister, but as we have seen, there he failed.

There were different reasons for his failure. Bo worked hard for his party. It was unthinkable for him to support any other party than the Social Democrats, and for many years he avoided criticizing it, since he saw no alternatives to it. Bo pushed its fundamental ideas: the ones in the party program—the ones which the party easily chose to forget in its ambition to remain in power—and he did it because he believed in them. He gave speeches in many places, on May Day and on other occasions, to local audiences: people who it was easier to communicate with than with the top party hierarchy. The latter gave him nothing in return for his efforts. Bo was no run-of-the-mill MP. His background differed visibly—and audibly—from that of the average Social Democratic parliamentarian. Bo had his own platform. He was an economics professor who possessed a much stronger analytical ability than the vast majority of his colleagues in Parliament, and he made use of it, thinking that it would be natural that the Social Democratic group would listen to what he had to say. It didn't. If we are to believe his own words, independent thinking was not hard currency in his party. It was the upper echelons in the party hierarchy that made all the decisions. Bo could never accept that. He never managed to subordinate himself to the party discipline and did not cherish the fact that his own pet ideas were not accepted by those who called the shots within the party.

Bo's personal characteristics did not serve him well either. At times they turned into an outright obstacle. He was a bad tactician and had to pay the price for this. His way of impatiently throwing out derogatory remarks in situations where he perceived that the party line was stupid made the party leadership consider him a back bencher who should not be allowed to step forward, let alone to influence the party stance on important issues.

In the end, Bo turned his back on the party and left Parliament.

A Convinced Provocateur

Bo was extremely interested in economic and social issues. This made him become an economist and an avid writer. There is no doubt that he was a genuine social reformer. He did not fight only for himself and his own position in society, but he also wanted common people to have a better life. They should be able to read good books and travel. In his heart, Bo was a reformist Social Democrat, all his life. He never praised the bourgeois parties, but whatever change that would occur in Sweden would have to be engineered by the Social Democrats, a party with many defects which Bo exposed, but still, for him, the only possible agent of change. No other party had achieved anything. In spite of all his critical remarks about the Social Democracy, he remained true to its core ideas, ideas which a party leadership mainly intent on staying in power had failed to realize.

Bo's critical stance toward his own party made his debate articles after he left Parliament hot stuff, easy to get published. In that sense, he was unique. He had the ability to stand up and analyze society from a point of view that nobody else in the party shared, because it brought no immediate political advantages. He combined his insider perspective with his analytical ability and a large dose of boldness. This appealed to many citizens. He was frequently approached by people who wanted to talk with him because they supported his ideas. His appeal lasted for several years. Bo kept writing newspaper articles for almost two decades after he left Parliament. With time, however, as it became clear that he was gradually becoming an outside critic, the media interest in him began to fade and his influence on the debate waned.[8]

Bo had problems refraining from emptying his poison glands when he wrote. He had an outspoken penchant for extravagant formulations—formulations which frequently hurt. Bo was a popular educator—very pedagogical—in his writings. He was a debater, but even more a provocateur. He made systematic use of provocations to bring his message across. As the amount of criticism he received for his articles eloquently testifies, the method was efficient. During his career, he first attacked the Social Democrats from the left, and then from the right. An article about him in *Dagens Nyheter* received the title "Kritiker som alltid gått i otakt" ("A Critic Always Out of Step").[9] Having said this, however, it is impossible to deny that Bo was filled by an irresistible desire to debate all kinds of issues which he considered important and where he felt that his party had gone wrong.

It was no coincidence that, in 1989, Bo received the Z Prize, a prize that was awarded annually between 1988 and 1991, by the *Z* magazine, owned by the successful and controversial businessman Jan Stenbeck and his Kinnevik company. The prize sum was 50,000 Swedish kronor and

---

[8] For a summary account of Bo's writings for DN Debatt, see Bergstrand (2011).
[9] Söderberg (1991).

was awarded to "persons who have highlighted other views and courses of events than the ones that usually feature in the press and the broadcasting media, who have given evidence of the possession of one or more of the following qualities: courage, integrity, meticulousness, good stylistic ability or verbal skills, objectivity and humor."[10] Bo got the prize for his "lack of conformity and tactical considerations. He has in many contributions to the debate of important issues created a much greater ceiling height than what is common in the friggebods [friggebodar] of Swedish politics."

The Z Prize diploma

The Intellectual

Bo Södersten was a pronounced intellectual. That always stood out when you spoke with him. He was well-read, in many genres, and he willingly shared his *Lesefrüchte* in his publications. He brought his children to hundreds of museums and made sure that they were properly exposed to history and fiction. Out of twelve Christmas gifts, eleven would regularly be

---

[10] Wikipedia (2019).

books. Bo also took great care to increase the cultural level of his students, discussing literature, art, and music with them. He recommended them to read widely on all kinds of subjects, not only economics.

Bo's intellectual disposition is present everywhere in his writings, especially in his essays. His four books of essays present a *mélange* of economic, political and literary themes on a general, popular level. The best of them is *Den hierarkiska välfärden*. It is a "real" book of essays where the ideas are in focus, and he demonstrates his ability to find topics that matter, be they economic, political, or literary. It is also the book where you feel that you are getting closest to the person Bo Södersten. He changed his political views later in life, but that is not the thing. *Den hierarkiska välfärden* is written by a man of flesh and blood. It was the first book that he gave to me and when I opened it, I immediately felt it: This was a book by a man with a burning conviction—a conviction which he managed to convey to the reader. The essay genre was ideal for his way of thinking: often an ideologically inspired idea that was applied to an author or some phenomenon in society.

This side of Bo unfortunately faded into the background over time, as political themes and economic policy took over, with one exception: the essay about Björn Larsson. Unfortunately, Bo did not quite deliver on his early promise. The following collections of essays are more ephemeral, with the exception of *Ut ur krisen*, where he collected some of his more important contributions. Wholesale writing in daily newspapers has its price.

All his life, Bo was an avid fiction reader: essays, novels, short stories, and biographies, but also poetry. Since he came from Dalarna, Erik Axel Karlfeldt was a favorite. He would occasionally quote him. Bo's number one idol, however, was of a much later date: Gunnar Ekelöf, of the generation of the 'forties. And he read Americans like Ezra Pound and Edgar Lee Masters. The first time Bo was on television was when he presented and discussed a play by the future Nobel laureate Harold Pinter, an author to the left of the British Labour Party, who shared his own Socialist convictions. Bo had the collected works of Bertolt Brecht, presumably mainly because Brecht was a radical, but he never spoke much about German culture. After having studied in France, he had become a Francophile and often spiced his conversation with phrases in French: "Les Français parlent trop." "Les Français réagissent lentement."

Bo also ventured into writing fiction himself. That he loved the genre was beyond doubt. It was enough with a quick tour of the Södersten library. He repeatedly demonstrated his ability to comment and criticize fiction. But that was not enough. He wanted to be part of the literary parnassus himself. His admiration of Björn Larsson probably to a large extent was due to the fact that the latter managed both to be a successful academic and an outstanding fiction writer. But criticizing and writing fiction are two different genres, and unfortunately you have to conclude that in Bo's own case the result was not convincing.

The Sybarite

Bo had regular work habits. He went to bed around 9.30 in the evening and read for half an hour before going to sleep, and he rose early in the morning to go to work. Most of what he wrote was produced before noon. He was, however, no ascetic, denying himself the pleasures of this world. On the contrary, Bo lived a sybaritic life. This did not only include women and culture, but home decoration, clothing, food, and drink as well. His taste for interior decoration was impeccable. Over the years he accumulated a number of works mainly by well-known Swedish artists. Clothes were also an important part of life. Already in the 1960s, Bo's suits were made to measure. He wanted to be a sharp dresser and could spend large amounts of money to demonstrate that he was one, "probably one of the few chairmen of Laboremus who had their suits tailor-made."[11] Exquisite food also had a prominent place in Bo's world. He enjoyed going to good restaurants with first-class menus, but his taste was firmly anchored in the Swedish kitchen. He liked the traditional type of home cooking with a bit of French flair. Enjoying food was a matter of quality.

Good food goes with good beverages. In his youth, Bo was a teetotaler. He did not taste any alcoholic drinks before the age of 27. However, he subsequently made up for his error by keeping a well-stocked wine cellar, the contents of which he generously shared with his guests. Cognac was his favorite drink—later in life occasionally too much of it—and he was never happier than when he could relax after dinner on the lawn of the family summer house in Kåseberga on the southern tip of Sweden with a glass of cognac and a cigar, looking at the surroundings in a state of perfect bliss.

[11] Milton (2011), p. 23.

Enjoying the good life. (Courtesy Anna Södersten Bengtsson)

Bo stayed in good physical shape—remained young—for many years. In his youth he had played football and practiced track and field. He and I played squash for several years, and he participated regularly in the economics department football team and in that of the Social Democrats during his period in Parliament. However, in 1995, he got diverticulitis and had to be hospitalized. Complications ensued: multiple organ failure after a failed operation, broken sutures, and the temporal use of a stoma. In the process he lost over 15 kilos of weight. This unfortunately reduced his mobility. He got scared of further complications, and henceforth abstained from physical activities and began to put on weight.

The Purpose of Life

Which were Bo's goals in life? Was he a man who sought power? Once he said to me that the finest Harvard chair was worth nothing in comparison with the most insignificant ministerial portfolio. Or did he want to become a celebrity? He was a bit of lens louse. Sometimes he argued that it didn't matter what you were doing. "The main thing is to keep your name in vogue." But why? What did he want to achieve? It felt a bit like when the popular Swedish actor Edvard Persson entered the film studio: "All the lights on me!" Was it therefore that he wrote all those newspaper articles? The headlines about him were far from always merciful and seldom laudatory. When the journalists found out something about him that they thought smelled scandal—house deals, tax planning—they put wartime headings on the placards. However, you cannot get away from the fact that Bo had a phenomenal nose for controversial issues—issues that he both believed to be important and which could be used to put himself into the limelight.

How did Bo perceive himself? There were moments when you easily could feel that he was suffering from a monumental overestimation of himself, a trait which surfaced not least when he had lost some race for a chair and appealed. He had been an A student and must hence when he arrived in Uppsala have been equipped with a cemented self-confidence, which he continued to document during the rest of his life. Bo was never weak in his faith. He had successfully done his bit of social climbing and could even speak about people as "real working class." He knew that he had left it himself and wanted to distance himself. On one occasion, I was in his office when he phoned for a flight ticket: "It's Professor Bo Södersten, I am also a Member of Parliament."

Still, he could not get away from his social background. He of course took advantage of it during his years in politics. It was no disadvantage for him to be Wiktor's son, the son of a Social Democrat and labor union leader beyond reproach. He was also proud of having made it in life, but had he really made it to the end station on the social ladder? Did he feel comfortable? Not necessarily, not all the time. Bo was an elitist, but his conception of elite built exclusively on his strong belief in meritocracy, and he had nothing but contempt for the arrogance displayed by certain people who were born on the top rung of the social ladder. Leaving one class does not guarantee that you are wholeheartedly accepted by another, and when Bo sensed that, he became suspicious and demanded what he felt was proper treatment and could go out of his way to get it.

How deep-seated was Bo's ideology? There remains no doubt that the roots were deep. He had been born into the labor movement and the Social Democracy. During his youth and way into his manhood he stood out as a radical hardcore Socialist—never in the revolutionary phrasemonger camp—that was on the other side of the demarcation line—but with time, he made an about turn and began his persistent criticism of the Social Democrats and their policies. In one respect, however, Bo was a convinced ideologue for a rather long period. When the idea of the labor-managed firm appeared, he immediately swallowed the bait. This was his great revelation in life and he did all that he could to launch the idea in

Sweden. It did not go well. The trade unions never thought of the idea as valuable. It was possible to launch the wage-earners' funds without labor management. The idea had sprung from abstract economic theory, not from the experience of the labor movement.

* * *

Bo's last years were not good. Those of us who met him more or less regularly could note a slow deterioration. Gradually, he began to lose touch with the conversation and drifted into his own world. In 2006, he began an examination of his mental faculties, and on 11 April 2008, he was diagnosed with Alzheimer's disease. In 2013, he moved into Riddargården, one of the best dementia nursing homes in Stockholm. It is located five minutes' walk from the Stockholm School of Economics, so I did my best to visit him regularly during his journey into the dark. Receiving visits cheered him up, and we always found something to talk about as long as his condition admitted it. Bo died on 5 September 2017.

Bo Södersten in a sense was larger than life. He was the kind of person that everybody loved to tell stories about, half of which cannot be printed. Perhaps the best summary of Bo was made by his long-time friend Villy Bergström, a man who never went around in circles but always spoke his mind. "Bo can be absolutely devilish," he said, "but it is impossible not to like him."

REFERENCES

Åhnberg, Annika (1999), *Isprinsessa*. Stockholm: Hjalmarson & Högberg
Andersen, Bent Rold (1972), Sakkunnigutlåtande vid tillsättningen av professuren i arbetsmarknadspolitik vid Institutet för social forskning vid Stockholms universitet. 23 October
Andersson, Sten (1993), *I de lugnaste vattnen*. Stockholm: Tiden
Arvidsson, Guy (1970), Sakkunnigutlåtande rörande ledigförklarad professur i nationalekonomi vid Göteborgs universitet (Aug Röhss' professur). 29 October
Asimakopoulos, Athanasios (1966), Review of *A Study of Economic Growth and International Trade*. By B. Södersten, *Economic Journal*, Vol. 76, No. 301, 100–102
Barrett, Nancy och Södersten, Bo (1975), 'Unemployment Flows, Welfare and Labor Market Efficiency in Sweden and the United States', *Swedish Journal of Economics*, Vol. 77, No. 3, 199–302
Bege (1977), 'Löntagarpengar i företaget säkrar ökat medinflytande', *Sundsvalls Tidning*, 2 May
Bentzel, Ragnar; Lindbeck, Assar and Ståhl, Ingemar (1963), *Bostadsbristen: En studie av prisbildningen på bostadsmarknaden*. Stockholm: Almqvist & Wiksell
Bergqvist, Anita (1993), 'Är professorns nonsensord närande men vård av sjuka och gamla tärande?', *Västerbottens Folkblad*, 13 February
Bergstrand, Mats (2011), 'DN Debatt i tid och otid', in: Mats Lundahl (ed.), *Den orädde debattören: En vänbok till Bo Södersten på 80-årsdagen den 5 juni 2011*. Stockholm: Ekerlids Förlag

Bergström, Hans (1997), 'Stärk demokratin och medborgerligheten!', *Dagens Nyheter*, 21 December

Björklund, Anders; Edin, Per Anders; Holmlund, Bertil and Wadensjö, Eskil (1994), 'Ekonomikollegor vilseleder', *Dagens Nyheter*, 14 October

Carlson, Benny and Lundahl, Mats (2019), *Ett forskningsinstitut expanderar: IUI från 1950 till 1966*. Stockholm: Ekerlids Förlag

Caves, Richard E. and Jones, Ronald W. (1973), *World Trade and Payments: An Introduction*. Boston: Little, Brown and Company

Chipman, John S. (1966), 'A Survey of the Theory of International Trade: Part 3, The Modern Theory', *Econometrica*, Vol. 34, No. 1, 18–76

Ehrenkrona, Olof (1991), *Nicolin: en svensk historia*. Stockholm: Timbro

Eidem, Rolf and Viotti, Staffan (1974), 'Arbetarstyrda företag i en marknadsstyrd ekonomi', *Ekonomisk Debatt*, Vol. 2, No. 3, 166–172

Ekberg, Jan; Södersten, Bo; Hammarstedt, Mats and Rooth, Dan-Olof (2002), 'Hårdare tag mot invandrare att vänta', *Dagens Nyheter*, 22 April

Ekdal, Niklas (2003), 'Apropå snyltgäster', *Dagens Nyheter*, 30 December

Ekholm, Karolina and Södersten, Bo (2002), 'Growth and Trade vs. Trade and Growth', *Small Business Economics*, Vol. 19, No. 2, 147–162

Erixon, Lennart and Wadensjö, Eskil (2013), 'Gösta Rehn (1913–96)—en otålig samhällsreformator', *Ekonomisk Debatt*, Vol. 40, No. 8, 71–82

Feldt, Kjell-Olof (1991), *Alla dessa dagar—: i regeringen 1982–1990*. Stockholm: Norstedts

Findlay, Ronald (1981), 'The Fundamental Determinants of the Terms of Trade', in: Sven Grassman och Erik Lundberg (red), *The World Economic Order: Past and Prospects*. London: Macmillan

Findlay, Ronald and Grubert, Harry (1959), 'Factor Intensities, Technological Progress, and the Terms of Trade', *Oxford Economic Papers*, Vol. 11, No. 1, 111–121

Flam, Harry (1980), 'En proklamation om handelskrig', *Dagens Nyheter*, 8 November

Fornäs, Johan; Hultén, Britt; Hvitfelt, Håkan; Kleberg, Madeleine; Lindhoff, Håkan; Mårtenson, Bo; Nowak, Kjell; Pollack, Ester and Thurén, Torsten (1998), 'Expertstyret slutar i despoti', *Dagens Nyheter*, 8 January

Franck, Anders (1977), 'Frälsningsläror hotar forskningen', *Göteborgs-Posten*, 11 February

Fransson, Jan; Johansson, Anita; Persson, Anita; Silfverstrand, Bengt and Södersten, Bo (1981), *Rapport från studieresa i Östtyskland och Frankrike 21–27 juli 1981*. October. Mimeo

Friedman, Milton and Friedman, Rose D. (1998), *Two Lucky People: Memoirs*. Chicago and London: University of Chicago Press

Friggebo, Birgit (2011), 'Friggeboden', i: Mats Lundahl (ed.), *Den orädde debattören: En vänbok till Bo Södersten på 80-årsdagen den 5 juni 2011*. Stockholm: Ekerlids Förlag

Furåker, Bengt (1994), 'Försörjning och marknad', *Ekonomisk Debatt*, Vol. 22, No. 4, 433–439

Galbraith, John Kenneth (1958), *The Affluent Society*. New York: Mentor

Galbraith, John Kenneth (1967), *The New Industrial State*. Boston: Houghton Mifflin

Gårdlund, Torsten (1939), *Frankrikes väg: ekonomi och socialpolitik 1918–1939*. Stockholm: Tidens Förlag

Gårdlund, Torsten (1942), *Industrialismens samhälle*. Stockholm: Tidens Förlag

Gårdlund, Torsten (1956), *Knut Wicksell. Rebell i det nya riket*. Stockholm: Bonniers

Gårdlund, Torsten (1958), *The Life of Knut Wicksell*. Stockholm: Almqvist & Wiksell

Gårdlund, Torsten (1965), *Att arbeta i u-land*. Stockholm: Wahlström & Widstrand

Gårdlund, Torsten (1967), *Lamco i Liberia*. Stockholm: Almqvist & Wiksell

Gårdlund, Torsten (1968), *Främmande investeringar i u-land*, Stockholm: Almqvist & Wiksell

Gårdlund, Torsten (1976), *Marcus Wallenberg 1864–1943: hans liv och gärning*. Stockholm: P.A. Norstedt & Söners Förlag

Gelting, Jørgen; Haavelmo, Trygve; Hoffmeyer, Erik; Ølgaard, Anders; and Nørregaard Rasmussen, P. (1969), Til det rets- och statsvidenskabelige fakultet ved Københavns Universitet. 19 June

Gustafsson, Karl-Erik (2017), *På Stigs tid. Familjen Hamrin & Jönköpings-Posten 1970–2007*. Stockholm: Ekerlids Förlag

Hansson, Göte (ed.) (1993), *Trade, Growth and Development: The Role of Politics and Institutions. Proceedings of the 12th Arne Ryde Symposium, 13–14 June 1991, in Honour of Bo Södersten*. London and New York: Routledge

Heckscher, Eli F. (1919), 'Utrikeshandelns verkan på inkomstfördelningen. Några teoretiska grundlinjer', *Ekonomisk Tidskrift*, Vol. 21, No. 2, 1–32

Heckscher, Eli F. (1991), 'The Effect of Foreign Trade on the Distribution of Income', in: Harry Flam and M. June Flanders (eds), *Heckscher-Ohlin Trade Theory*. Cambridge, MA and London: MIT Press

Hedwall, Barbro (1995), 'Produktivitet, sa professorn', *Expressen*, 3 May

Hicks, John R. (1953), 'An Inaugural Lecture', *Oxford Economic Papers*, Vol. 5, No. 2, 117–135

Hobsbawm, Eric J, (1994) *Age of Extremes: The Short Twentieth Century 1914–1991*. London: Michael Joseph

Horvat, Branko (1974), 'Om teorin för arbetarstyrda företag', *Ekonomisk Debatt*, Vol. 2, No. 2, 83–87

Hultkrantz, Lars och Österholm, Pär (eds), *Marknad och politik*. Tolfte upplagan. Lund: Studentlitteratur

Imperial Ethiopian Government, Ministry of Public Health (1973), *Health Sector Review (Draft), Fourth Five-Year Plan*. Addis Ababa: Ministry of Public Health, 17 April

Jalakas, Anne (1994), 'Södersten tänker om', *Arbetet*, 31 October

Janson, Svante (1995), 'Bo Södersten måste avgå', *Dagens Nyheter*, 4 May

Johansson, Anders L (1992), *Gunnar Sträng: landsvägsagitatorn*. Stockholm: Tidens förlag

Johansson, Östen and Jungenfelt, Karl G. (1964), Review of *A Study of Economic Growth and International Trade* by Bo Södersten, *Ekonomisk Tidskrift*, Vol. 66, No. 3, 222–230

Johnson, Harry G. (1955), 'Economic Expansion and International Trade', *Manchester School of Economic and Social Studies*, Vol. 23, No. 2, 95–112

Jonasson, Erik; Pettersson, Lars and Södersten, Bo (2005), 'Spåren av amatörernas framfart är förskräckande', *Dagens Nyheter*, 9 August

Jones, Ronald W. (1969), 'Tariffs and Trade in General Equilibrium: Comment', *American Economic Review*, Vol. 59, No. 3, 418–424

Joyce, James (1914), *Dubliners*. London: Grant Richards

Karyd, Arne and Södersten, Bo (1990), 'The Swedish Housing Market from a Distributional Perspective: Market and Policy Interactions', in: Inga Persson (ed.), *Generating Equality in the Welfare State: The Swedish Experience*. Oslo: Norwegian University Press

Kemp, Murray C. (1964), Book Review: *A Study of Economic Growth and International Trade*. By Bo Södersten. *American Economic Review*, Vol. 54, No. 6, 1157–1158

Keynes, John Maynard (1912), 'Tables Showing for Each of the Years 1900–1911 the Estimated Value of Foreign Trade of United Kingdom at Prices of 1900', *Economic Journal*, Vol. 22, No. 88, 630–631

Kokk, Enn (n.d.), 'Södersten, Bo: Övertygelser', http://enn.kokk.se/?page_id=612. Downloaded 5 March 2022

Krugman, Paul R. and Obstfeld, Maurice (1987), *International Economics: Theory and Policy*. Glenview, IL: Little, Brown

Kruse, Agneta and Ståhlberg, Ann-Charlotte (2020), 'Pensionsreformen 1994— ett kvarts sekel senare', *Ekonomisk Debatt*, Vol. 49, No. 7, 19–27

Larsson, Björn (1980), *Splitter*. Stockholm: Wahlström & Widstrand

Larsson, Björn (1992), *Den keltiska ringen*. Stockholm: Bonniers

Larsson, Björn (1995), *Long John Silver*. Stockholm: Norstedts

Larsson, Björn (1997), *Drömmar vid havet*. Stockholm: Norstedts

Larsson, Björn (1999a), *Det onda ögat*. Stockholm: Norstedts

Larsson, Björn (1999b), *Le capitaine et les rêves*. Paris: Éditions Grasset

Leijon, Anna-Greta (1991), *Alla rosor ska inte tuktas!* Stockholm: Tiden

Lewin, Leif (1988), *Det gemensamma bästa: om egenintresset och allmänintresset i västerländsk politik*. Stockholm: Carlssons

Lewis, W. Arthur (1954), 'Economic Development with Unlimited Supplies of Labour', Vol. 22, No. 2, 139–191
Lewis, W. Arthur (1969), *Aspects of Tropical Trade 1883–1965*. Stockholm: Almqvist & Wiksell
Lindbeck, Assar (1969a), Sakkunnigutlåtande vid tillsättningen av professur i nationalekonomi vid juridiska fakulteten vid Uppsala universitet. 29 March
Lindbeck, Assar (1969b), Till Juridiska fakulteten vid Lunds universitet, 19 November
Lindgren, Anne-Marie (1978), 'Fel lösningar på fel problem', *Tiden*, Vol. 70, No. 5, 245–249
Lönnroth, Johan (2011), 'Han var trots allt nog ganska nyttig för oss', in: Mats Lundahl (ed.), *Den orädde debattören: En vänbok till Bo Södersten på 80-årsdagen den 5 juni 2011*. Stockholm: Ekerlids Förlag
Lucas, Robert E. (1988), 'On the Mechanics of Economic Development', *Journal of Monetary Economics*, Vol. 22, No. 1, 3–42
Lucas, Robert E. (1990), 'Why Doesn't Capital Flow from Rich to Poor Countries?', *American Economic Review*, Vol. 80, No. 2, 92–96
Lundahl, Mats (ed.) (1981), *Ideologi, ekonomi och politik: Tankar i tiden*. Stockholm: Rabén & Sjögren
Lundahl, Mats (ed.) (2011), *Den orädde debattören: En vänbok till Bo Södersten på 80-årsdagen den 5 juni 2011*. Stockholm: Ekerlids Förlag
Lundahl, Mats and Södersten, Bo (1974a) 'Forskning för utveckling', *Ekonomisk Debatt*, Vol. 2, No. 2, 115–122
Lundahl, Mats and Södersten Bo (eds) (1974b), *Utvecklingsekonomi 1: Underutvecklingens mekanismer*. Stockholm: Aldus
Lundahl, Mats and Södersten, Bo (eds) (1974c), *Utvecklingsekonomi 2: Planering och resursmobilisering*. Stockholm: Aldus
Lundahl, Mats and Södersten Bo (eds) (1979), *Utvecklingsekonomi*. Andra, reviderade upplagan. Stockholm: Aldus
Lundahl, Mats and Södersten, Bo (2000), 'Cuba i den halvhjärtade marknadsekonomins år', *Ekonomisk Debatt*, Vol. 28, No. 7, 669–680
Lundahl, Mats and Södersten, Bo (2004), 'Ekonomporträtt: Torsten Gårdlund—en *grandseigneur*', *Ekonomisk Debatt*, Vol. 32, No. 8, 47–60
Lundahl, Mats and Södersten, Bo (2009a), *Torsten Gårdlund: Det goda livets ekonom*. Stockholm: Timbro
Lundahl, Mats and Södersten, Bo (2009b), 'Torsten Gårdlund—ett porträtt', in: Mats Lundahl, *Fem svenska ekonomer: Knut Wicksell, Eli Heckscher, Bertil Ohlin, Torsten Gårdlund, Staffan Burenstam Linder. Vad skev de egentligen?* Stockholm: Timbro
Lundahl, Mats and Södersten, Bo (2010), 'Essäisten Torsten Gårdlund', in: *Vid kapitalismens sjukbädd och andra essäer. Texter av Torsten Gårdlund i urval av Mats Lundahl och Bo Södersten*. Stockholm: Timbro

Lundahl, Mats and Södersten, Bo (2015), 'Torsten Gårdlund: A Portrait', in: Mats Lundahl, *Seven Figures in the History of Swedish Economic Thought: Knut Wicksell, Eli Heckscher, Bertil Ohlin, Torsten Gårdlund, Sven Rydenfelt, Staffan Burenstam Linder and Jaine Behar*. Houndmills, Basingstoke and New York: Palgrave Macmillan

Lundberg, Erik (1972), Sakkunnigutlåtande vid tillsättningen av professuren i arbetsmarknadspolitik vid Institutet för social forskning vid Stockholms universitet. 31 October

Lundgren, Nils (2011), 'Bo, Herbert och jag—en slitstark relation', in: Mats Lundahl (ed.), *Den orädde debattören: En vänbok till Bo Södersten på 80-årsdagen den 5 juni 2011*. Stockholm: Ekerlids Förlag

MacKenzie, Norman (ed.) (1958), *Conviction*. London: MacGibbon & Kee

Magnusson, Lars (1996), *Sveriges ekonomiska historia*. Stockholm: Rabén Prisma

Magnusson, Lars (2007), *An Economic History of Sweden*. London and New York: Routledge

Mäler, Karl-Göran and Södersten, Bo (1967), 'Factor-Biased Technical Progress and the Elasticity of Substitution', *Swedish Journal of Economics*, Vol. 69, No. 2, 154–160

Meade, James E. (1964), *Efficiency, Equality and the Ownership of Property*. London: George Allen & Unwin

Metzler, Lloyd A. (1949a), 'Tariffs, the Terms of Trade, and the Distribution of National Income', *Journal of Political Economy*, Vol. 57, No. 1, 1–29

Metzler, Lloyd A. (1949b), Tariffs, International Demand, and Domestic Prices', *Journal of Political Economy*, Vol. 57, No. 4, 345–351

Milton, Anders (2011), 'Morbror Bo', in: Mats Lundahl (ed.), *Den orädde debattören: En vänbok till Bo Södersten på 80-årsdagen den 5 juni 2011*. Stockholm: Ekerlids Förlag

Milton, Anders and Södersten, Bo (1996), 'Sverige har för många läkare'", *Dagens Nyheter*, 24 December

Motion till riksdagen 1987/1988: Bo 208, om stödet till bostadsbyggande. Bo Södersten and Roland Sundgren. https://data.riksdagen.se/fil/C9F849B0-3252-41FA-A8DC-528000367BB4. Downloaded 22 September 2021

Myrdal, Alva and Myrdal, Gunnar (1934), *Kris i befolkningsfrågan*. Stockholm: Albert Bonniers förlag

Myrdal, Gunnar (1953), *The Political Element in the Development of Economic Theory*. London: Routledge & Kegan Paul

Myrdal, Gunnar (1968), *Asian Drama: An Inquiry Into the Poverty of Nations*. 3 Volumes. New York: The Twentieth Century Fund

Myrdal, Gunnar (1972), *Vetenskap och politik i nationalekonomin*. Ny omarbetad upplaga. Stockholm: Rabén & Sjögren

Neuberger, Egon (1965), Review of Södersten, Bo, *A Study of Economic Growth and International Trade*, Kyklos, Vol. 17, No. 2, 389–391

Nordh, Sture och Pettersson, Torbjörn (1995), 'En manlig krigsförklaring', *Dagens Nyheter*, 10 May

Notat (1977), Notat til møte 31. januar 1977 i 'tjänsteförslagsnämnden för samhällsvetenskapliga fakulteten vid Lunds universitet'. January

Ohlin, Bertil (1922), *Det interregionala bytets teori*. Stockholm: Licentiate thesis, Stockholms Högskola (Stockholm College)

Ohlin, Bertil (1924), *Handelns teori*. Stockholm: AB Nordiska Bokhandeln

Ohlin, Bertil (1933), *Interregional and International Trade*. Cambridge, MA: Harvard University Press

Ohlin, Bertil (1969a), 'Internationell ekonomi', *Sydsvenska Dagbladet Snällposten*, 3 October

Ohlin, Bertil (1969b), 'Ohlin svarar Södersten', *Sydsvenska Dagbladet Snällposten*, 17 October

Ohlin, Bertil (1991), *The Theory of Trade*, in: Harry Flam and M. June Flanders (eds), *Heckscher-Ohlin Trade Theory*. Cambridge, MA and London: MIT Press

Ohlin, Bertil (2002), 'The Theory of Interregional Exchange', in: Ronald Findlay, Lars Jonung and Mats Lundahl (eds), *Bertil Ohlin: A Centennial Celebration (1899–1999)*. Cambridge, MA and London: MIT Press

Ølgaard, Anders (1970), Sakkunnigutlåtande rörande ledigförklarad professur i nationalekonomi vid Göteborgs universitet (Aug Röhss' professur). 1 November

Olson, Mancur (1965), *The Logic of Collective Action: Public Goods and the Theory of Groups*. Cambridge, MA and London: Harvard University Press

Palander, Tord (1969), Sakkunnigutlåtande vid tillsättningen av professur i nationalekonomi vid juridiska fakulteten vid Uppsala universitet. 18 May

Persson, Inga and Södersten, Bo (1971), *Internationella resursfördelningsproblem. Nationalekonomi 5*. Stockholm: Svenska Utbildningsförlaget Liber AB

Pettersson, Ulla (1994), 'Varför ser ingen att Södersten är naken?', *Dagens Nyheter*, 25 August

Prebisch, Raúl (1950), *The Economic Development of Latin America and Its Principal Problems*. New York: United Nations

Riksdagens protokoll 1987/88:110, 28 April 1988. https://data.riksdagen.se/fil/612D884E-9D69-4EAD-AEE7-5E7429342937. Downloaded 22 September 2021

Romer, Paul M. (1986), 'Increasing Returns and Long-Run Growth', *Journal of Political Economy*, Vol. 94, No. 5, 1002–1037

Romer, Paul M. (1990a), 'Endogenous Technological Change', *Journal of Political Economy*, Vol. 98, No. 5, 70–102

Romer, Paul M. (1990b), 'Are Nonconvexities Important for Understanding Growth?', *American Economic Review*, Vol. 80, No. 2, 97–103

Rothstein, Bo and Boëthius, Maria-Pia (1993), 'Ekonomernas kåranda tystar kritiken', *Dagens Nyheter*, 1 March
Rybczynski, T.M. (1955), 'Factor Endowments and Relative Commodity Prices', *Economica*, NS, Vol, 22, No. 88, 336–341
Sandelin, Bo (1977), *Prisutveckling och kapitalvinster på bostadsfastigheter*. Göteborg: Nationalekonomiska institutionen vid Göteborgs universitet
Sandelin, Bo and Södersten, Bo (1978), *Betalt för att bo: Värdestegring och kapitalvinster på bostadsmarknaden*. Stockholm: Rabén & Sjögren
Schön, Lennart (2000), *En modern svensk ekonomisk historia. Tillväxt och omvandling under två sekel*. Stockholm: SNS Förlag
Singer, Hans (1950), 'The Distribution of Gains between Borrowing and Lending Countries, *American Economic Review*, Vol. 40, No. 11, 473–485
Sjöström, Hans O. (1987), *Klassens ljus eller hur man hamnar i arbetarregeringen*. Stockholm: Norstedts
Skidelsky, Robert (1995) *The World after Communism: A Polemic for Our Times*. Houndmills, Basingstoke: Macmillan
Söderberg, Karen (1991), 'Kritiker som alltid gått i otakt', *Dagens Nyheter*, 5 January
Södersten, Bo (n.d.), *Kandidaterna*. Unpublished novel manuscript
Södersten, Bo (1959a), *Studier i den långsiktiga utvecklingen av svensk utrikeshandel*. Mimeo. Uppsala: Nationalekonomiska institutionen vid Uppsala universitet
Södersten, Bo (1959b), 'Utrikeshandel och ekonomisk utveckling', *Ekonomiska Samfundets Tidskrift*, Vol. 12, 276–288
Södersten, Bo (1959c), Paulus och den fria konkurrensen', *Libertas*, Vol. 19, No. 6, 7–9
Södersten, Bo (1960), 'Socialisering. Opopulära tankegångar i en inaktuell fråga', *Tiden*, Vol. 52, No. 3, 145–148
Södersten, Bo (1961), 'Utrikeshandel och ekonomisk tillväxt: den marginella aspekten', *Ekonomisk Tidskrift*, Vol. 63, No. 2, 115–128
Södersten, Bo (1962a), *Övertygelser*. Stockholm: Albert Bonniers Förlag
Södersten, Bo (1962b), 'Foreign Trade and Economic Growth: The Marginal Aspect', *International Economic Papers*, No. 11, 185–195
Södersten, Bo (1962c), 'Den nya dollarkrisen', *Ekonomisk Tidskrift*, Vol. 64, No. 1, 1–21
Södersten, Bo (1963), "Bostadsbristen och de tre räntorna", *Tiden*, Vol. 55, No. 5, 292–301
Södersten, Bo (1964a), *A Study of Economic Growth and International Trade*. Stockholm: Almqvist & Wiksell
Södersten, Bo (1964b), 'Svar på Johansson-Jungenfelts recension', *Ekonomisk Tidskrift*, Vol. 66, No. 4, 299–303
Södersten, Bo (1968a), 'Kuba i det heroiska Vietnams år', *Tiden*, Vol. 60, No. 9, 548–558.

Södersten, Bo (1968b), *Den hierarkiska välfärden och andra essäer.* Stockholm: Rabén & Sjögren

Södersten, Bo (1969a), *Internationell ekonomi.* Stockholm: Rabén & Sjögren

Södersten, Bo (1969b), 'Öppet brev till Bertil Ohlin', *Sydsvenska Dagbladet Snällposten*, 9 October

Södersten, Bo (1969c), Till den juridiska fakulteten vid Lunds universitet. 3 November

Södersten, Bo (1970a), *International Economics.* London och Basingstoke: Macmillan

Södersten, Bo (ed.) (1970b), *Svensk ekonomi.* Stockholm: Rabén & Sjögren

Södersten, Bo (1970c), 'Per Albin och den socialistiska reformismen', in: Gunnar Fredriksson, Dieter Strand and Bo Södersten, *Per Albinlinjen: Tre ställningstaganden till en socialdemokratisk tradition.* Stockholm: Bokförlaget PAN/ Nordstedts

Södersten, Bo (1971a), 'För lite politik', *Arbetet*, 13 January

Södersten, Bo (1971b), 'Reallön som partsinlaga', *Dagens Nyheter*, 26 February

Södersten, Bo (1972), 'Assar Lindbecks liberala teser', *Aftonbladet*, 21 March

Södersten, Bo (1973a), 'Arbetarstyrd ekonomi', *Ekonomisk Debatt*, Vol. 1, No. 8, 479–490

Södersten, Bo (1973b), 'Nationalekonomi', in: *Presentationer av ämnesområden utgivna i samband med Göteborgs universitets professorsinstallation lördagen den 20 oktober 1973.* Göteborg: Informationssekretariatet vid Göteborgs universitet

Södersten, Bo (ed.) (1974a), *Svensk ekonomi.* Andra omarbetade och utökade upplagan. Stockholm: Rabén & Sjögren

Södersten, Bo (1974b), 'Rapport från juntans Chile', *Aftonbladet*, 23 February

Södersten, Bo (1974c), 'Juntans väg till makten', *Aftonbladet*, 25 February

Södersten, Bo (1974d), 'Allendes tragedi: Det går inte att utrota fattigdomen på några år', *Aftonbladet*, 3 March

Södersten, Bo (1974e), 'Inkomstfördelningen som globalt problem', *Tiden*, Vol. 66, No. 1, 5–13

Södersten, Bo (1975), *Den svenska sköldpaddan: Politiskt, ekonomiskt, personligt ur ett socialdemokratiskt perspektiv.* Stockholm: Rabén & Sjögren

Södersten, Bo (1976a), *Economia internazionale.* Torino: Unione Tipografico-Editore Torinense

Södersten, Bo (1976b), 'Mikroaspekter av löntagarstyre', *Ekonomisk Debatt*, Vol. 4, No. 1, 30–41

Södersten, Bo (1976c), 'Manifest över svikna ambitioner', *Tiden*, Vol. 68, No. 2, 109–122

Södersten, Bo (1976d), 'Den sanna pluralismen: Teser om löntagarstyre', *Tiden*, Vol. 68, No. 4–5, 197–209

Södersten, Bo (1977a), 'Arbetarna får dra lasset', *Arbetet*, 16 April

Södersten, Bo (1977b), 'Löntagarna måste få styra investeringar(na)', 17 April

Södersten, Bo (1977c), 'Det borgerliga krispaketet', *Tiden*, Vol. 69, No. 7, 431–441
Södersten, Bo (1978a), *Internationell ekonomi*. Andra omarbetade upplagan. Stockholm: Rabén & Sjögren
Södersten, Bo (1978b), 'Kvinnan på arbetsmarknaden', *Ekonomisk Debatt*, Vol. 6, No. 8, 598–606
Södersten, Bo (1979a), *Economia internacional*. Rio de Janeiro: Editora Interciencia
Södersten, Bo (1979b), 'Mot ett löntagarstyrt Sverige?', in: Villy Bergström and Bengt Rydén (eds), *Vägval i svensk politik. Ekonomi och samhälle på 80-talet*. Stockholm: SNS Förlag
Södersten, Bo (1980a), *International Economics*. Second edition. London: Macmillan
Södersten, Bo (1980b), 'Frihandeln bör begränsas', *Dagens Nyheter*, 22 October
Södersten, Bo (1980c), 'New Attitudes to Work', in: Edmond Malinvaud and Jean-Paul Fitoussi (eds), *Unemployment in Western Countries: Proceedings of a Conference Held by the International Economic Association at Bischenberg, France*. London: Macmillan
Södersten, Bo (1981a), *Ut ur krisen: Kortsiktiga lösningar och långsiktiga mål i svensk politik*. Stockholm: Rabén & Sjögren
Södersten, Bo (1981b), 'Comments to "The Fundamental Determinants of the Terms of Trade", by Ronald Findlay', in: Sven Grassman and Erik Lundberg (eds), *The World Economic Order: Past and Prospects*. London: Macmillan
Södersten, Bo (ed.) (1982a), *Svensk ekonomi*. Tredje omarbetade upplagan. Stockholm: Rabén & Sjögren
Södersten, Bo (1982b), 'Towards a Labor-Managed Sweden?', in: Bengt Rydén and Villy Bergström (eds), *Sweden: Choices for Economic and Social Policy in the 1980s*. London: George Allen & Unwin
Södersten, Bo, under medverkan av Lennart Berg, Sten Magnusson och Bo Sandelin (1983), *Makroekonomi och stabiliseringspolitik*. Lund: Liber Förlag
Södersten, Bo (1984a), 'Vi skall inte förblindas av revolutionsromantik', *Svenska Dagbladet*, 21 January
Södersten, Bo (1984b), 'Ogrundad myt om kuppen 1973', *Svenska Dagbladet*, 4 March
Södersten, Bo (1984c), 'Absurd ekonomisk situation', *Svenska Dagbladet*, 7 March
Södersten, Bo (1984d), 'Palatset eller kyrkogården', *Svenska Dagbladet*, 15 March
Södersten, Bo (1985a), *A külgazdaság hatásmechanizmusa*. Budapest: Közgazdasági és Jogi Könyvkiadó
Södersten, Bo (1985b), 'Mineral-Led Development: The Political Economy of Namibia', in: Mats Lundahl (ed.), *The Primary Sector in Economic Development: Proceedings of the Seventh Arne Ryde Symposium, Frostavallen, August 29–30 1983*. London and Sydney: Croom Helm

Södersten, Bo (1985c), 'Bevarad standard?', *Göteborgs-Posten*, 13 May
Södersten, Bo (1985d), 'Sverige sämst i klassen 1986', *Dagens Industri*, 6 November
Södersten, Bo (1986), 'Socialdemokratin behöver en slav på vagnen', *Svenska Dagbladet*, 26 July
Södersten, Bo (ed.) (1987a), *Marknad och politik: Strukturer och problem i svensk ekonomi*. Lund: Dialogos
Södersten, Bo (1987b), 'Ryck upp universiteten!', *SACO-Tidningen*, No. 4, 30–31
Södersten, Bo (1987c), 'Utför från välfärdstoppen', *Dagens Nyheter*, 5 July
Södersten, Bo (1988a), 'Tänk om i familjepolitiken!', *Dagens Nyheter*, 24 January
Södersten, Bo (1988b), 'Vi behöver mer pragmatism i mitten', *Dagens Industri*, 30 May
Södersten, Bo (1988c), 'Revor i ädelhetens fana', *Dagens Nyheter*, 5 June
Södersten, Bo (1988d), 'Ta chansen att dra in på folk', *Dagens Industri*, 20 October
Södersten, Bo (1988e), 'Makten är något som gärna döljs', *Aktuellt i politiken*. Reprinted in Södersten. Bo (1991), *Kapitalismen byggde landet*. Stockholm: SNS Förlag
Södersten, Bo (ed.) (1989a), *Skattereform och skatteplanering: Vårt nya skattesystem i funktion*. Lund: Dialogos
Södersten, Bo (1989b), 'Skattereformens politiska ekonomi', in: Bo Södersten (ed.), *Skattereform och skatteplanering: Vårt nya skattesystem i funktion*. Lund: Dialogos
Södersten, Bo (1989c), 'Systemfel i bostadspolitiken', in: Ds 1989:47, *Bostadsstödet—alternativ och konsekvenser. Bidrag till ett seminarium anordnat av Expertgruppen för Studier i offentlig ekonomi*. Stockholm: Allmänna Förlaget
Södersten, Bo (1989d), 'Populister skapar privilegier', *Dagens Nyheter*, 2 July
Södersten, Bo (1989e), 'Systemfelens överstepräster', *Dagens Nyheter*, 13 August
Södersten, Bo (1989f), 'Senarelägg avvecklingen', *Dagens Nyheter*, 17 August
Södersten, Bo (1989g), 'Inga utfästelser om förtida avveckling', *Dagens Nyheter*, 8 September
Södersten, Bo (1989h), 'Skandalen i Lund', *Sydsvenska Dagbladet Snällposten*, 13 November
Södersten, Bo (1989i), 'Låt Arken leva', *Sydsvenska Dagbladet Snällposten*, 30 November
Södersten, Bo (1989j), 'Stöd Vietnams väg mot marknadsekonomi', *Svenska Dagbladet*, 27 December
Södersten, Bo (ed.) (1990a), *Marknad och politik*. 2:a reviderade upplagan. Lund: Dialogos
Södersten, Bo (ed.) (1990b), *Den stora reformen: Handbok om de nya skatterna*. Stockholm: SNS Förlag
Södersten, Bo (ed.) (1990c), *Framtid med kärnkraft*. Stockholm: SNS Förlag

Södersten, Bo (1990d), 'Cien años de desarrollo económico sueco (1870–1970)', in: Magnus Blomström and Patricio Meller (eds), *Trayectorias divergentes. Comparación de un siglo de desarrollo económico latinoamericano y escandinavo*. Santiago de Chile: CIEPLAN-Hachette

Södersten, Bo (1990e), 'Estado, sociedade e mercado: Um estudio sobre experiências suecas', *Finisterra—Revista de Reflexâo e Crítica*, No. 6, 111–123

Södersten, Bo (1990f), 'Ljus framtid för Chile', *Svenska Dagbladet*, 29 January. Reprinted in *Kapitalismen byggde landet*

Södersten, Bo (1990g), 'Orimligt ge Chile bistånd', *Dagens Nyheter*, 30 January

Södersten, Bo (1990h), 'Carlsson i LO:s ledband', *Expressen*, 7 February

Södersten, Bo (1990i), 'Ett parti utan ledning', *Dagens Nyheter*, 5 May

Södersten, Bo (1990j), 'Kapitalismen byggde landet', *Dagens Nyheter*, 2 August

Södersten, Bo (1990k), 'Ni har lovat att ta ner månen', *Dagens Nyheter*, 22 August

Södersten, Bo (1990l), 'Krispaketet håller inte', *Dagens Nyheter*, 27 October

Södersten, Bo (1990m), 'Gör högskolan konsumentstyrd', *Sydsvenska Dagbladet Snällposten*, 13 December

Södersten, Bo (1991a), 'One Hundred Years of Swedish Economic Development', in: Magnus Blomström and Patricio Meller (eds), *Diverging Paths; Comparing a Century of Scandinavian and Latin American Economic Development*. Washington, DC: Inter-American Development Bank

Södersten, Bo (1991b), 'Sverige—dårarnas paradis', *Dagens Nyheter*, 27 January

Södersten, Bo (1991c), 'Södersten, Bo (1991c), S skapade ett klassamhälle', *Dagens Nyheter*, 28 January

Södersten, Bo (1991d), 'Skugga över Hongkong', *Sydsvenska Dagbladet Snällposten*, 31 January

Södersten, Bo (1991e), 'Marknaden—inte bara hans förtjänst', *Svenska Dagbladet*, 15 April

Södersten, Bo (1991f), 'Kjell-Olof Feldt och öppenheten', *Svenska Dagbladet*, 23 April

Södersten, Bo (1991g), 'Därför är vi så rika', *Dagens Nyheter*, 28 April

Södersten, Bo (1991h), 'Groteskt högskolesystem', *Dagens Nyheter*, 8 July

Södersten, Bo (1991i), 'Var hamnar makten?', *Sydsvenska Dagbladet Snällposten*, 23 September

Södersten, Bo (1991j), 'Sparande, tillväxt och internationellt beroende', in: *Bankmöte 91. Anföranden och diskussion vid Bankmötet den 6 november 1991*. Stockholm: Svenska Bankföreningen

Södersten, Bo (1991k), 'Anna-Greta Leijons fall från makten', *Svenska Dagbladet*, 11 November

Södersten, Bo (1991l), *Kapitalismen byggde landet*. Stockholm: SNS Förlag

Södersten, Bo (ed.) (1992a), *Pendeln svänger—röster i högskoledebatten*. Stockholm: SNS Förlag

Södersten, Bo (ed.) (1992b), *Den offentliga sektorn*. Stockholm: SNS Förlag

Södersten, Bo (1992c), 'Det svenska pensionssystemet', in: Bo Södersten (ed.), *Den offentliga sektorn*. Stockholm: SNS Förlag
Södersten, Bo (1992d), 'Därför går det så illa', *Dagens Nyheter*, 3 January
Södersten, Bo (1992e), 'Yrkesgrupper utan berättigande', *Dagens Nyheter*, 4 January
Södersten, Bo (1992f), 'Tusen diligenser gör ingen järnväg', *Svenska Dagbladet*, 15 April
Södersten, Bo (1992g), 'Regeringen faller sönder', *Dagens Nyheter*, 17 May
Södersten, Bo (1992h), 'De svaga länkarnas regering', *Dagens Nyheter*, 18 May
Södersten, Bo (1992i), 'Möblera om bland ministrarna', *Dagens Nyheter*, 21 December
Södersten, Bo (1993a), 'Institutions, Knowledge, Trade and Growth: A Personal Address', in: Göte Hansson (ed.), *Trade, Growth and Development: The Role of Politics and Institutions*. Proceedings of the 12th Arne Ryde Symposium. 13–14 June 1991, in Honour of Bo Södersten. London and New York: Routledge
Södersten, Bo (1993b), 'Gunnar Sträng—en folkets man', *Svenska Dagbladet*, 10 February
Södersten, Bo (1993c), 'Bromsklossen Westerberg', *Dagens Nyheter*, 7 March
Södersten, Bo (1993d), 'Välfärdsstatens tid är förbi', *Dagens Nyheter*, 20 June
Södersten, Bo (1993e), 'Politiska minnen i anekdotens form', *Svenska Dagbladet*, 15 September
Södersten, Bo (1993f), 'Efter oss syndafloden', *Sydsvenska Dagbladet Snällposten*, 12 October
Södersten, Bo (1993g), 'Hur går det med ATP?', *Sydsvenska Dagbladet Snällposten*, 29 November
Södersten, Bo (1993?), *Riksdagens minskade makt—myt eller verklighet?* Unpublished address
Södersten, Bo (1994a), *Knowledge, Economic Progress and the State. Anförande av professor Bo Södersten vid Utbildningsdepartementets internationella symposium 'Science and the Powers' den 16–17 mars på Hässelby slott*. Stockholm: SULF
Södersten, Bo (1994b), 'Män mest missgynnade', *Dagens Nyheter*, 4 January
Södersten, Bo (1994c), 'M och s måste samarbeta', *Dagens Nyheter*, 5 January
Södersten, Bo (1994d), 'Ned med utgifterna', *Sydsvenska Dagbladet Snällposten*, 21 February
Södersten, Bo (1994e), 'I väntan på IMF', *Sydsvenska Dagbladet Snällposten*, 20 June
Södersten, Bo (1994f), 'Hur kunde det gå så snett?', *Dagens Nyheter*, 9 August
Södersten, Bo (1994g), 'Sverige idag i djupare beråd än någonsin', *Svenska Dagbladet*, 20 September
Södersten, Bo (1994h), 'Kris och förnöjsamhet', *Sydsvenska Dagbladet Snällposten*, 3 October
Södersten, Bo (1994i), 'Flykt från verkligheten', *Sydsvenska Dagbladet Snällposten*, 12 December

Södersten, Bo (1995a), 'Politisk korruption förstör landet', *Dagen Nyheter*, 28 January
Södersten, Bo (1995b) 'Esclavage fiscal. Gaspillage et corruption politique détruisent la Suède', *Courrier International*, No. 224
Södersten, Bo (1995c), 'Kvinnor har för höga löner', *Dagens Nyheter*, 30 April
Södersten, Bo (1995d), 'Ner i godtyckets träsk', *Svenska Dagbladet*, 26 May
Södersten, Bo (1995e), 'Från Lenin till Sahlin', *Sydsvenska Dagbladet Snällposten*, 25 September
Södersten, Bo (1995f), 'Pensionssystem i fara', *Dagens Nyheter*, 22 November
Södersten, Bo (ed.) (1996a), *Marknad och politik*. Tredje upplagan. Stockholm: SNS Förlag
Södersten, Bo (1996b), 'Carlsson huvudansvarig för krisen', *Dagens Nyheter*, 3 January
Södersten, Bo (1996c), 'Palme var en svag ledare', *Dagens Nyheter*, 3 March
Södersten, Bo (1996d), 'Nedskärningar bra för kvinnor', *Dagens Nyheter*, 13 July
Södersten, Bo (1996e), 'Inkompetenskult inom s', *Dagens Nyheter*, 11 August
Södersten, Bo (1996f), 'Dömda till misär', *Sydsvenska Dagbladet Snällposten*, 25 November
Södersten, Bo (1996g), 'Fattiga kusiner', *Sydsvenska Dagbladet Snällposten*, 30 December
Södersten, Bo (ed.) (1997a), *Marknad och politik*. Fjärde upplagan. Stockholm: SNS Förlag
Södersten, Bo (1997b), 'De hundra lysande åren i svensk ekonomi', *Svenska Dagbladet*, 7 January
Södersten, Bo (1997c), 'S-gruppen svag och undfallande', *Dagens Nyheter*, 18 February
Södersten, Bo (1997d), 'Lär av Tony Blair', *Sydsvenska Dagbladet Snällposten*, 16 June
Södersten, Bo (1997e), 'S måste låta marknaden styra', *Dagens Nyheter*, 12 August
Södersten, Bo (1997f), 'Kollektivet före individen', *Sydsvenska Dagbladet Snällposten*, 17 September
Södersten, Bo (1997g), 'Begränsa demokratin!', *Dagens Nyheter*, 14 December
Södersten, Bo (1998a), 'Röveri mot gamla och sjuka', *Dagens Nyheter*, 1 April
Södersten, Bo (1998b), 'Facket i vågskålen', *Sydsvenska Dagbladet Snällposten*, 6 April
Södersten, Bo (1998c), 'Metallbasen LO:s svagaste ledare', *Dagens Nyheter*, 7 August
Södersten, Bo (1998d), 'Milton Friedman är högerns svar på Keynes', *Svenska Dagbladet*, 3 September
Södersten, Bo (1998e), 'Göran Persson ett problem för s', *Dagens Nyheter*, 24 September
Södersten, Bo (1998f), 'Låt förtidspensionärer återgå i arbete', *Dagens Nyheter*, 28 November

Södersten, Bo (1999a), 'Goda institutioner bakom västs framgång', *Svenska Dagbladet*, 6 May
Södersten, Bo (1999b), 'Statligt översitteri saboterar pensionen', *Dagens Nyheter*, 22 May
Södersten, Bo (1999c), 'Särintresset kräver företräde', *Svenska Dagbladet*, 28 June
Södersten, Bo (1999d), 'Slarva inte bort även denna högkonjunktur', *Svenska Dagbladet*, 11 August
Södersten, Bo (1999e), 'Ohlin framför Myrdal', *Sydsvenska Dagbladet Snällposten*, 18 October
Södersten, Bo, (1999f), 'Annika Åhnbergs memoarer', *Jönköpings-Posten*, 4 November
Södersten, Bo (ed.) (2000a), *Marknad och politik. Femte upplagan*. Stockholm: SNS Förlag
Södersten, Bo (2000b), 'Många politiker är inte vana vid kritik', *Avisen*, 29 July
Södersten, Bo (2000c), 'Folkhemmets trygghetssystem hotar välfärden', *Svenska Dagbladet*, 3 November
Södersten, Bo (2000/2001), 'Björn Larsson djuplodar de sju haven', *Moderna Tider*, No. 122/123, December/January, 68–69
Södersten, Bo (2001a), *Unpublished draft of memoirs*. Manuscript
Södersten, Bo (2001b), 'Usel integration', *Sydsvenska Dagbladet Snällposten*, 26 February
Södersten, Bo (2001c), 'Attacs recept har gett armod på Kuba', *Dagens Nyheter*, 14 April
Södersten, Bo (2001d), 'Ekonomipriset tappar sin betydelse', *Dagens Nyheter*, 10 December
Södersten, Bo (2002a), 'Fram med sakfrågorna', *Sydsvenska Dagbladet Snällposten*, 8 April
Södersten, Bo (2002b), 'Svenska modellen fungerar inte', *Dagens Nyheter*, 24 July
Södersten, Bo (2002c), 'Mindre avund, tack', *Sydsvenska Dagbladet Snällposten*, 12 November
Södersten, Bo (2003a), 'Hymla inte om invandrare", *Dagens Nyheter*, 28 December
Södersten, Bo (2003b), 'På resa med EWK', in: Berit Skogsberg (ed.), *EWK: En liten vänbok till en stor mästare*. No place: EWK-sällskapet
Södersten, Bo (ed.) (2004a), *Globalization and the Welfare State*. Houndmills, Basingstoke and New York: Palgrave Macmillan
Södersten, Bo (2004b), 'The Welfare State as a General Equilibrium System', in: Bo Södersten, (ed.), *Globalization and the Welfare State*. Houndmills, Basingstoke and New York: Palgrave Macmillan
Södersten, Bo (2004c), 'Malmö på efterkälken', *Sydsvenska Dagbladet Snällposten*, 29 January
Södersten, Bo (2004d), 'Chockerande siffror om förtidspension', *Dagens Nyheter*, 12 February

Södersten, Bo (2004e), 'Grön återvändsgränd', *Sydsvenska Dagbladet Snällposten*, 2 October
Södersten, Bo (2004f), 'Förutfattad bild av USA', *Sydsvenska Dagbladet Snällposten*, 30 October
Södersten, Bo (2005a), 'Reform Failure and Poor Economic Performance: The Case of Sweden', in: Mats Lundahl and Michael L Wyzan (eds), *The Political Economy of Reform Failure*. London and New York: Routledge
Södersten, Bo (2005b), 'En ohållbar ordning', *Sydsvenska Dagbladet Snällposten*, 9 April
Södersten, Bo (2005c), 'Svårt att bevara välfärdsstaten', *Sydsvenska Dagbladet Snällposten*, 11 May
Södersten, Bo (2005d), 'En fråga om attityd', *Sydsvenska Dagbladet Snällposten*, 17 June
Södersten, Bo (2005e), 'Tillväxt utan jobb', *Sydsvenska Dagbladet Snällposten*, 3 November
Södersten, Bo (ed.) (2006a), *Den problematiska tryggheten—välfärdsstaten under tre decennier*. Stockholm: SNS Förlag
Södersten, Bo (2006b), 'Tre decennier med den svenska välfärdsstaten', in: Bo Södersten (ed.), *Den problematiska tryggheten—välfärdsstaten under tre decennier*. Stockholm: SNS Förlag
Södersten, Bo (2006c), 'Det goda exemplet Indien', *Sydsvenska Dagbladet Snällposten*, 19 July
Södersten, Bo and Nyberg, Kristian (2001), 'Trettio år av chilensk ekonomi', *Ekonomisk Debatt*, Vol, 29, No. 5, 347–358
Södersten, Bo and Reed, Geoffrey (1994), *International Economics*. Third edition. Houndmills, Basingstoke och London: Macmillan
Södersten, Bo and Söderström, Hans Tson (eds) (2004), *Marknad och politik*. Sjätte upplagan. Stockholm: SNS Förlag
Södersten, Bo and Vind, Karl (1968), 'Tariffs and Trade in General Equilibrium', *American Economic Review*, Vol. 58, No. 3, 394–408
Södersten, Bo and Vind, Karl (1969), 'Tariffs and Trade in General Equilibrium: Reply', *American Economic Review*, Vol. 59, No. 3, 424–426
Solow, Robert M. (1956), 'A Contribution to the Theory of Economic Growth', *Quarterly Journal of Economics*, Vol. 70, No. 1, 65–94
SOU 1973:41, *Forskning för utveckling. Betänkande avgivet av U-landsforskningsberedningen*. Stockholm: Utbildningsdepartementet. Göteborgs Offsettryckeri
Stolper, Wolfgang and Samuelson, Paul A. (1941), 'Protection and Real Wages', *Review of Economic Studies*, Vol. 9, No 1, 58–73
Sundell, Ingegerd (1993), 'Närande och tärande', *Nya Norrland*, 12 February
Swedberg, Richard (1991), *Joseph A, Schumpeter: His Life and Work*. Cambridge: Polity Press

Tingsten, Herbert (1961), *Mitt Liv: Ungdomsåren*. Stockholm: Wahlström & Widstrand
Tingsten, Herbert (1962), *Mitt Liv: Mellan trettio och femtio*. Stockholm: P.A. Norstedt & Söners förlag
Tingsten, Herbert (1963), *Mitt Liv: Tidningen 1946–1952*. Stockholm: P.A. Norstedt & Söners förlag
Tingsten, Herbert (1964), *Mitt Liv: Tio år 1953–1963*. Stockholm: P.A. Norstedt & Söners förlag
Tobisson, Lars (1971), 'Söderstens nidbild', *Dagens Nyheter*, 1 March
Torrens, Robert (1821), *An Essay on the Production of Wealth*. London: Longman, Hurst, Orme, Brown & Green
Vanek, Jaroslav (1970), *The General Theory of Labor-Managed Economies*. Ithaca, NY and London: Cornell University Press
Werin, Lars (1972), Sakkunnigutlåtande vid tillsättningen av professuren i arbetsmarknadspolitik vid Institutet för social forskning vid Stockholms universitet. 30 October
Widmalm, Sten (2019), 'De integrationspolitiska utredningarna som kulturkrig', *Respons*, Vol. 12, No. 6, 19–25
Wikipedia (2019), 'Z (tidning)', 15 November. https://sv.wikipedia.org/wiki/Z_(tidning). Downloaded 8 March 2022
Ytterberg, Claes-Bertil (1997), 'Södersten legitimerar nazism', *Dagens Nyheter*, 22 December

Index[1]

A
Aarhus, 45, 46
Abel-Smith, Brian, 16n14
The Affluent Society, 37
Africa, 81–82, 141, 77
Aftonbladet, 59, 60, 78, 85, 93, 152
Age of Extremes: The Short Twentieth Century 1914–1991, 137
Åhnberg, Annika, 139
Aktuellt i Politiken, 125
Alla dessa dagar (*All These Days*), 138
Allende, Salvador, 78–81
Alzheimer's disease, 141, 161
American Economic Review, 26, 30
American University in Washington, DC, 50, 78
Andersen, Bent Rold, 49
Andersson, Sten, 87, 138, 139
Annales school, 137
Arken preschool, 115
Arvidsson, Guy, 46, 47

Asia, 82–83
Asimakopoulos, Athanasios, 27
Asmussen, Svend, 5
Association Internationale des Étudiants en Sciences Économiques et Commerciales (AIESEC), x
ATP pension system, 101, 110–112
August Röhss chair in economics, 45, 46
Austria, 31

B
Balance of payments, 11, 20, 33, 34, 70, 79, 80, 95
Baltic states, 120
Barrett, Nancy, 49, 78
Barsebäck, 114
Basque Country, 66
Becker, Gary, 50

---

[1] Note: Page numbers followed by 'n' refer to notes.

© The Author(s), under exclusive license to Springer Nature Switzerland AG 2022
M. Lundahl, *Bo Södersten from Left to Right*, Palgrave Studies in the History of Economic Thought,
https://doi.org/10.1007/978-3-031-09101-8

Bentzel, Ragnar, 9, 12, 24, 37n2, 45–47, 53
Berg, Lennart, 70
Bergstrand, Mats, xi, 145n1
Berkeley, 19, 29, 32
Betalt för att bo (*Paid for Dwelling*), 53, 56
Bildt, Carl, 101
Bostadsbristen: En studie av prisbildningen på bostadsmarknaden (*The Housing Shortage: A Study of Price Formation in the Housing Market*), 24
"Bostadsbristen och de tre räntorna" ("The Housing Shortage and the Three Rents"), 24
Botswana, 81, 147
Bourdet, Yves, xi, 145n1
Bourgeois parties in Sweden, 43, 101, 155
Braconier, Henrik, xi, 145n1
Brotherhood, 42–44, 62
Brunnsvik folk high school, 1

C
Calder, Nigel, 16n14
Capital formation, 43, 59–62, 93
Capitalism, 38, 39, 59, 60, 62, 92, 93, 99, 153
Carlsson, Henry, *see* Ramqvist, Henry
Carlsson, Ingvar, 87, 126, 131, 132
Cassel, Gustav, 94
Castro, Fidel, 77, 78, 80
Catching culture, 121–123
Caves, Richard, 19, 35
Center for Latin American Development Studies at Boston University, x
Centralization, 44, 61, 67, 127
Chicago, 140

Chile, 77–81, 140, 147
China, 74, 78
Chipman, John, 35
Christian Democratic Party in Sweden, 101
CIB Corporation, x
Committee on Reformed Income Taxation (Kommittén för reformerad inkomstbeskattning [RINK]), 86
Communism, 60, 77, 80, 82, 83, 115, 137, 139
Concentration of power, 125–129, 131
Conservatism, 42, 44, 96, 102
Conservative Party in Sweden, 42, 44
Conviction, 16, 37
Copenhagen, 23, 46, 146
Cornell University, 59
Corruption, 125–129
Costa Rica, 77, 81
Cuba, 77–80, 147

D
Dagens Nyheter, 40, 41, 91, 99, 107, 134, 155
Dalarna, 1, 85, 87, 157
Danish National Bank, 46
Daycare centers, 115
Den hierarkiska välfärden (*The Hierarchic Welfare*), 37, 39–41, 92, 157
Denmark, 45, 47, 50, 103, 119, 135
Den offentliga sektorn (*The Public Sector*), 111
Den problematiska tryggheten – välfärdsstaten under tre decennier (*The Problematic Security – the Welfare State During Three Decades*), 134

Den stora reformen (*The Great Reform*), 106
Den svenska sköldpaddan (*The Swedish Turtle*), 61, 92
Det gemensamma bästa (*The Common Good*), 97
Developing countries, 19, 23, 23n16, 26, 35, 69–77, 82, 147
Dickson, Harald, 45
Docent, 25, 29, 47
Doctoral dissertation, x, 19–24, 27, 46, 53, 118, 142, 152
Doi moi, 82
Dubliners, 16
Duvalier, François (Papa Doc), 78

E
Eastern Europe, 77, 119, 137
EC, 31
Economic growth in Sweden, 2, 3, 10, 31, 35, 39, 46, 56, 59, 61, 64–66, 69, 70, 72–74, 79, 80, 82, 87, 95, 99, 102–104, 107, 121, 127, 131, 134, 136, 152
Economic Journal, 27
Economic policy, 42, 48, 52, 70, 71, 78–81, 87, 94–97, 101, 103, 132, 138, 152, 157
EEC, 31, 33
Efficiency, Equality and the Ownership of Property, 40n6
Ehrenkrona, Olof, 138
Eidem, Rolf, 66
Ekholm, Karolina, xi, 31, 145n1
Ekonomisk Debatt, 73, 141
Ekonomisk Tidskrift, 19, 25
Elasticity factor, 22
Employment, 23, 33, 40, 48, 64, 65, 70, 77, 85, 86, 103, 104, 110, 113, 120–122, 134, 136

EMU, 31, 72
England, 40
Eriksson, Gunnar, xi, 6, 25, 145n1
Essays, 16, 24, 37–44, 48, 61, 62, 65, 75, 78, 81, 85, 92, 94, 95, 99, 141–143, 153, 157
An Essay on the Production of Wealth, 23
Ethiopia, 81
European Union (EU), 31, 72, 119, 120, 136
EWK (Ewert Karlsson), 78, 141

F
Factor price equalization theorem, 21, 32, 140
Feldt, Kjell-Olof, xi, 42, 89, 90, 138, 139, 145n1
Findlay, Ronald, 20, 21, 22n13, 23n16
Finisterra—Revista de Reflexão e Crítica, 76
Finland, 119, 146
Flam, Harry, 87
Folkhemmet (The People's Home), 42
Ford Foundation, 29
Framtid med kärnkraft (*A Future with Nuclear Power*), 114
France, 31, 40, 79, 142, 157
Fredriksson, Gunnar, xi, 42
Friedman, Milton, 140
Friedman, Rose, 140
Frielingsdorf Lundqvist, Helena, xi, 145n1, 147
Frielingsdorf, Per-Axel, xi, 145n1, 147
Friggebo, Birgit, xi, 91, 92, 145n1, 147, 148
Furåker, Bengt, 109

G

Galbraith, John Kenneth, 37, 39
Gårdlund, Torsten, x, xi, 29, 51, 141–143, 152
GATT, 33
Gelting, Jørgen, 45–47
Germany, 135
Gislaved, 123
Globalization and the Welfare State, 134, 136
Gnosjö, 123
Göteborgs-Posten, 51
Gothenburg, x, 45–48, 50–53, 78, 109, 119, 121, 146, 151
Government Committee on Capital Gains, 86
Grängesberg, 1, 6
Grappelli, Stéphane, 5
Great Britain, 31, 135
Greece, 79, 110, 121
Greeley, Horace, 29
Green Party in Sweden, 97, 101, 102, 106, 115
Green Revolution, 75
Growth of Swedish GDP, 2, 10, 31, 70, 104, 119, 120, 122
Growth theory, 75
Grubert, Harry, 20, 21
Gustafsson, Hans, 88

H

Haavelmo, Trygve, 46
Haavisto, Tarmo, xi, 70n2
Haiti, x, 77, 78
Hannerberg, David, 25
Hansson, Per Albin, 42–44
Harvard, 50, 159
Health care, 3, 81, 128, 132–134
Heckscher, Eli, 20, 35
Heckscher-Ohlin theorem, 21, 32, 34–35, 140

Hicks, John, 10n2, 20, 21, 29
High school, 1, 6, 25, 117, 146, 152
Hitler, Adolf, 128
Hobsbawm, Eric, 137
Hoffmeyer, Erik, 46
Hoggart, Richard, 16n14
Holland, 103, 133, 135
Hong Kong, 31, 82, 83
Hultkrantz, Lars, 72
"Hur kunde det gå så snett?" ("How Could It Get That Wrong?"), 122, 123

I

Idberg, Tobias, xi
IMF, 34
Income distribution, 32, 75, 76, 80, 95, 102
India, x, 82
Industrialismens samhälle (*Industrial Society*), 142
"Industripolitik för arbetarstyre" ("Industrial Policy for Labor Management"), 61
International Economics, ix, 32–36, 36n19, 47, 87, 152
Islam, 74

J

Japan, 31, 75
Johansen, Leif, 45
Johansson, Anders L., 139
Johansson, Göran, 121
Johansson, Östen, 22n12, 25
Johnson, Harry, 19–21
Johnson, Paul, 16n14
Jonasson, Erik, 103
Jones, Mervyn, 16n14
Jones, Ronald, 30, 35

Jönköping, 91, 147, 148, 151
Jönköping International Business School, 91, 134
Jönköpings-Posten, 91, 148
Jonung, Lars, xi, 141
Jorgenson, Dale, 19
Joyce, James, 16
Jungenfelt, Karl, 22n12, 25, 47

K
Kamali, Masoud, 121
Kandidaterna (The Students), 15
Kapitalismen byggde landet (Capitalism Built the Country), 92, 99
Karyd, Arne, 56
Kemp, Murray, 26, 29
Kennedy Round, 34
Keynes, John Maynard, 23, 137, 139, 140
Kindleberger, Charles, 19
Knut Wicksell. Rebell i det nya riket, 142
Kris i befolkningsfrågan (Crisis in the Population Question), 115
Krugman, Paul, 35
"Kvinnor har för höga löner" ("Female Wages Are Too High"), 132
Kyklos, 27

L
Laboremus, 12, 15, 85, 158
Labor-managed economy, 59–67, 153
Labor-managed firms, 59–65, 67, 85, 90, 95, 160
Larsson, Björn, 141, 157, 158
Laxtorp, 4
Lebanon, 121
Le capitaine et les rêves, 141

L'École des Sciences Politiques in Paris, 9
Left Party in Sweden, 102, 103, 115, 142
Leijon, Anna-Greta, 138, 139
Leipzig, 115
Leontief paradox, 32
Lewin, Leif, 97
Lewis, W. Arthur, 23n16
Liberalism, 39–41, 90
Liberal Party in Sweden, 42, 44, 90, 95, 147
Libertas, 13
Licentiate thesis, 9–12, 19, 46, 73, 152
The Life of Knut Wicksell, 142
Lindahl, Erik, 9
Lindbeck, Assar, 24, 25, 45–47, 53, 134
Lindgren, Anne-Marie, xi, 56n4
Lisbon, 76
LO, 127
London School of Economics, 9
Los Chicago Boys, 140
Ludvika, 6
Lund, x, 29, 32, 45, 50–52, 73, 91, 115, 123, 141–143, 146, 147, 150, 151
Lundberg, Erik, 25, 49
Lund University, ix, xi, 29

M
MacKenzie, Norman, 16n14
Magnusson, Lars, 137
Magnusson, Sten, 70
Makroekonomi och stabiliseringspolitik (Macroeconomics and Stabilization Policy), 70, 71
Malaysia, 31
Mäler, Karl-Göran, 29
Malmö, 119, 120

Marknad och politik (*Markets and Politics*), 71
Marris, Peter, 16n14
Marxism, 51
Marxists, xiii, 39, 50, 51, 51n17, 137
Meade, James, 40n6
Metal Workers Union, 133
Metzler, Lloyd, 30
Mexico, 77
Military service, 9, 146
Milton, Anders, xi, 133, 145n1
MIT, 19, 21
Mitt liv (*My Life*), 40
Moderate Party in Sweden, 101, 102
"Modern inflations-och arbetslöshetsteori" ("Modern Inflation and Unemployment Theory"), 48
Mondragón, 66
Murdoch, Iris, 16n14
Myrdal, Alva, 115
Myrdal, Gunnar, 94, 112, 140, xi, 25, 40, ix

N
Namibia, 81, 82
National Labour Market Board, 108, 129
NATO, 41
Neuberger, Egon, 27
New Democracy Party in Sweden, 101
The new dollar crisis, 20
New household economics, 50
The New Industrial State, 39
Nicaragua, 81
Nicolin, Curt, 138
Nixon, Richard, 140
Nobel, Alfred, 140
Nordic and Latin American countries, 47, 75, 78, 80, 81
Nørregaard Rasmussen, Poul, 46

Norrland, 104, 123
North, Douglass, 74
Nottingham University, 35
Nourishing and draining sectors, 106–110
Nuclear power, 95, 113–118
Nyberg, Kristian, 80
Nycander, Svante, xi
Nystroem, Gösta, 5
Nyström, Märtha, 5

O
Obstfeld, Maurice, 35
OECD, 96, 136
OEEC, 20
Ohlin, Bertil, 20, 34, 35, 93, 140
Ølgaard, Anders, 46, 47
Olsen, Erling, 23
Olson, Mancur, 61
Örnelius, Kristian, xi
Oslo, 23, 45, 46
Österholm, Pär, 72
Östlind, Anders, 24, 25
Övertygelser (*Convictions*), 16, 17, 41
Oxford, 20

P
Palander, Tord, 45, 46
Palme, Olof, 90, 127, 131
Paris, 9, 115
Parliament, x, xiii, xiv, 85–91, 94, 97, 101, 106, 115, 125–128, 131, 136, 139, 147, 151–155, 159, 160
"Paulus och den fria konkurrensen" ("Paul and Free Competition"), 13
Pendeln svänger—röster i högskoledebatten (*The Pendulum Swings—Voices in the University Debate*), 117

Pensions, 41, 80, 101,
  110–112, 111n21
Per Albinlinjen (*The Per Albin Way*), 42
Persson, Göran, 103, 120, 126
Persson, Inga, xi, 36n19, 145n1, 151
Petersson, Jeanie, xi, 145n1
Petersson, Lennart, xi, 145n1
Pettersson, Lars, xi, 103, 145n1
Pettersson, Ulla, 123
Pinochet, Augusto, 78–81, 140
Planering och resursmobilisering (*Planning and Resource Allocation*), 73
Poland, 120
Populism, 103, 131
Prebisch, Raúl, 23, 26
Preschools, 115
Prisutveckling och kapitalvinster på bostadsfastigheter (*Price Developments and Capital Gains in the Housing Market*), 53
Privata Affärer, 91
Prix Médicis étranger, 141
Public sector, 3, 69, 72, 94, 95, 101, 103–112, 121, 127, 129, 131–134, 136, 137
Puerto Rico, x

R
Ramqvist, Henry, 5
Ramqvist, Lars, xi, 5, 145n1
Real estate taxation, 54–56
Record years, 3
Reed, Geoffrey, 35
Reepalu, Ilmar, 120
Reformist Socialism, 44, 78
Regulated housing market, 56, 57
Rehn, Gösta, 49
Rents, 24, 54, 56, 57, 82
Riksbank, 2, 140

Rosenberg, Nathan, 74
Rosenstein-Rodan, Paul, x
Roskilde, 50
Roskilde University Centre, 50
Rybczynski, Tadeusz, 20–22, 32
Rybczynski theorem, 21, 22, 32
"Ryck upp universiteten!" ("Upgrade the Universities!"), 116
Rydén, Robert, xi

S
SACO (the Swedish Confederation of Professional Associations), 105
Sahlin, Mona, 121, 126
Sandberg, Nils-Eric, xi
Sandelin, Bo, xi, 53, 55, 70, 70n2, 145n1, 151
San Juan, x
Schumpeter, Joseph, 139
Scitovsky, Tibor, 19
Second World War, 3, 76
Serck-Hanssen, Jan, 51
Shore, Peter, 16n14
Singapore, 31
Singer, Hans, 23
Singer-Prebisch hypothesis, 23, 33
Sjöholm, Fredrik, xi, xiii, 145n1
Sjöström, Hans O., 12–14, 17, 27, 97, 148
Skattereform och skatteplanering (*Tax Reform and Tax Planning*), 106
Skidelsky, Robert, 137
Småland, 123
Social Democracy, xiii, 1, 2, 38, 41, 44, 76, 90, 93, 96, 99, 125, 127, 139, 155, 160
Social Democratic Party in Sweden, 3, 27, 44, 127, 131, 139
Socialism, xiii, 12, 17, 39, 40, 44, 59, 62, 78, 85, 153

"Socialismen på prov: fallet Chile" ("Socialism on Trial The Case of Chile"), 78
Socialist International, 40
"Socialpolitik och ekonomisk politik" ("Social Policy and Economic Policy"), 48
Södersten, Alice, 3–6
Södersten, Anna, xi, 2, 4, 14, 145n1, 146, 151
Södersten, Astrid, xi, 145n1, 146, 147, 151
Södersten, Erik, 3, 5, 6
Södersten, Greta, 3–6, 14
Södersten, Helge, 3, 4, 6
Södersten, Helmer, 3, 4
Södersten, Sigrid, 3–6
Södersten, Stig, 3–6
Södersten, Wiktor, xi, 1, 2, 4, 14, 145n1, 146, 160
Söderström, Hans Tson, 71
Solow, Robert M., 23n16
South Africa, 81, 82
South Korea, 31
Standing Committee on Finance, 85
Standing Committee on Taxation, 86
Stockholm School of Economics, x, 141, 142, 161
Stockholm University, 19, 45, 48, 128
Stolper-Samuelson theorem, 21, 30
Strand, Dieter, 42
A Study of Economic Growth and International Trade, 26
Svennilson, Ingvar, 19, 24, 25
Svenska Dagbladet, 91, 142
Svensk ekonomi (*The Swedish Economy*), 69, 73
Sveriges ekonomiska historia (*An Economic History of Sweden*), 137
Sveriges Riksbank Prize in Economic Sciences in Memory of Alfred Nobel, 140
Swaziland, 81, 147
Swedberg, Richard, 139
Sweden, xiii, 2, 3, 9, 10, 31, 38, 45, 47, 49–51, 53, 55, 64–66, 69–76, 80, 82, 87, 95–97, 99, 100, 103, 104, 107, 108, 110, 113–122, 125–129, 131–136, 138–139, 143, 146, 147, 155, 158, 161
  foreign trade, 9, 10, 20, 70, 86
Swedish Association of University Teachers—SULF, 116, 118
Swedish economic development, 73, 136
Swedish import capacity, 11, 31
Swedish industrialization, 75, 82, 96, 142
Swedish Institute for Social Research (Institutet för social forskning [SOFI]), 48–50
Swedish International Development Agency (SIDA), x, 73, 81
Swedish model, 3, 135
Swedish welfare system, 121–123, 136
Sydsvenskan, 91
Syria, 121
Systemic defects, 131–136

T
Taxation of housing, 55
Tax burden, 103, 104, 111, 122, 129, 136
Technical progress, 21–23, 25, 29, 30, 32, 39, 63, 71, 75
Terms-of-trade, 10, 11, 19–23, 21n10, 23n16, 30, 31, 33
Thalberg, Björn, 45–47
Tham, Carl, 118
Thomas, Hugh, 16n14

Thonstad, Tore, 23, 25, 51
Tiden, 12, 37, 55, 75, 77
Tingsten, Herbert, 40–42
Tobisson, Lars, 105
Torrens, Robert, 23
Townsend, Peter, 16n14
Trade unions, 1, 23, 44, 76, 96, 127, 132, 161
Tunisia, x, 29, 142
Turkey, 121

U
UNCTAD, 34
Underutvecklingens mekanismer (*The Mechanisms of Underdevelopment*), 73
"Unemployment Flows, Welfare and Labor Market Efficiency in Sweden and the United States," 49
United States, 19, 20, 31, 32, 49, 50, 96, 146
University of California, 19, 29
Uppsala, 6, 9–17, 45, 85, 89, 137, 146, 149, 152, 160
Utopian Socialists, 61, 143
Ut ur krisen (*Out of the Crisis*), 44, 92, 95, 157
Utvecklingsekonomi (*Development Economics*), 73

V
Vanek, Jaroslav, 59
Värnamo, 123
Västmanland, 1
Vetenskap och politik i nationalekonomin (*The Political Element in the Development of Economic Theory*), 93
Vietnam, 78, 82
Vind, Karl, 29, 30
Viotti, Staffan, 66

W
Wage-Earners' Funds, 64–66, 85, 95, 161
Waggeryd, 123
Wallenberg, Marcus, Sr., 142
Wedberg, Anders, 25
Welfare state, 3, 72, 76, 80, 108, 120, 122, 123, 132–136
Werin, Lars, 49
West Germany, 96
Williams, Raymond, 16n14
The World after Communism, 137
World Trade and Payments, 35

Y
Ytterberg, Claes-Bertil, 128
Yugoslavia, 66, 121

Printed in the United States
by Baker & Taylor Publisher Services